W.L. MARTIN
HOME DESIGNS™
VOLUME ONE

PUBLISHER	Dennis Brozak
ASSOCIATE PUBLISHER	Linda Reimer
EDITOR	Kevin Blair
PLANS EDITOR	Tina Leyden
DESIGNER	W.L. Martin
WRITER	Carol Stratman Shea
GRAPHIC DESIGNERS	Heather Guthrie
	Jeff Dedlow
	Mary Fitzmaurice
	Yen Gutowski
PRODUCTION ASSISTANT	Jeff Blair
RENDERING ILLUSTRATOR	Shawn Doherty
TECHNICAL ADVISERS	Carl Cuozzo
	Rob Phillips
CIRCULATION MANAGER	Priscilla Ivey

W.L. MARTIN
HOME DESIGNS™

IS PUBLISHED BY:
DESIGN BASICS PUBLICATIONS
11112 JOHN GALT BLVD., OMAHA, NE 68137
WEB - www.designbasics.com
E-MAIL - info@designbasics.com

CHIEF EXECUTIVE OFFICER	Dennis Brozak
PRESIDENT	Linda Reimer
DIRECTOR OF MARKETING	Kevin Blair
BUSINESS DEVELOPMENT	Paul Foresman
CONTROLLER	Janie Murnane
EDITOR-IN-CHIEF	Bruce Arant

Library of Congress Number: 99-075875
ISBN: 1-892150-18-2

W.L. MARTIN
HOME DESIGNS™

William Martin, president of W.L. Martin Home Designs,™ has been designing homes since 1983. His wide variety of experience in the home building industry, from engineering and estimating to his work as a general contractor have strongly influenced his design style and principles.

In 1986, he founded W.L. Martin Home Designs,™ designing homes for contractors and home buyers in northern Florida. During that time he also acquired his building license and for several years built, as well as designed homes. As the demand for his plans increased, he returned to designing exclusively. His design work soon dominated the local area.

In 1996, he relocated to Tulsa, Oklahoma and continued to design homes. By staying in one home no longer than a couple of years, Martin is still able to put his new ideas into practice through homes that he builds for himself. From his building experience, Martin recognizes the importance of striving for a balance between cost-effective construction methods and architectural creativity in home design. This is the underlying philosophy of all the homes he has created in this debut collection.

The development of any design says something about its creator.

It mirrors the designer's creativity, thought process, and perhaps most notably, what is important to the designer in the way a home should live.

At first glance, the homes of W.L. Martin reveal his commitment to a pleasing, traditional approach to design that complements a variety of architectural styles. From rooflines to windows, each elevation is easy on the eye and attractively balanced with just the right number of elements.

The elevation of a home is clearly important to Martin. Garages – especially three-car garages – are minimized through a variety of creative design techniques, channeling the emphasis on a home to its individual design style. In some cases, Martin places the garage to the rear, to avoid a distraction of the frontal view.

Martin's designs often feature places to entertain outdoors. Front and rear porches reveal his commitment to blurring the lines between interior and exterior living space. At a minimum, these spaces provide a quiet hideaway on a hectic day. Cost efficiency is clearly a part of Martin's design philosophy. Each design in this book was developed to help reduce expenses during construction of the home. Room sizes, as much as possible, are conducive to standard lumber lengths, which reduces job site waste. Many of the expensive elements on a home: foundation jogs, roof pitches and special detailing and trim are concentrated – though not exclusively – to the front of the home, where they will offer the most impact.

Many of Martin's designs are also controlled in terms of overall width and depth, to assist both builders and home buyers with selecting a home plan for some of today's narrower or more challenging home sites.

Places for children are also important to Martin, revealed through features like walk-in closets in most secondary bedrooms. And if a home's square footage will accommodate it, you'll find play areas, study areas or game rooms to keep toys out of sight or provide a getaway for the kids.

The goal in each of his homes, Martin says, is to "provide a place that feels much larger than its actual square footage." That translates to open areas, where two or three rooms feel like one large space. If open connection is not attained throughout all areas of the home, long views are shared between rooms strategically placed to attain a visual connection.

Though it's easy to see the common threads throughout Martin's work, his designs are far from mundane reproductions of the same idea. Each of the 53 home plans on the following pages offers its own advantages, amenities and appeal. Each is unique in its own right. From 1263 to 3914 square feet, designs in the W.L. Martin collection offer something for everyone.

One of my goals with one-story homes is to try to split the master suite from the secondary bedrooms whenever possible. That is a very popular feature with a lot of home buyers. However, for those who may have a small child or baby, I try to place a study within the vicinity of the master suite, so that it can be utilized as a nursery now and later converted into a study.

Another goal on one-story homes – and all my homes – is to try to cut hallway space to a minimum. In one-story homes, hallways can get too long in the attempt to offer some privacy to the bedrooms. By cutting down on hallway space, I can enlarge the other spaces in the home.

—W.L. Martin

Price Code 12

plan name **GLENCO**

plan number **#24045-9P**

This efficient one-story home relies on front and rear porches to offer additional living space outdoors.

- A vaulted ceiling and arched openings bring drama to the living room, which serves as the main living area of the home.

- A walk-in pantry is a welcome feature in the kitchen, which also offers an island counter and eating bar.

- The dining area has a comfortable atmosphere because of its openness to the kitchen and has a stunning view into the living room.

- A rear location for the master suite offers ideal privacy for relaxing in a soaking tub.

- A full bath and laundry room are steps from two additional bedrooms.

ORDER DIRECT
TOLL-FREE
(800) 947~7526

www.designbasics.com

CUSTOMIZE
any home plan

FINISHED SQ. FT.   1263

First Floor

© W. L. Martin Designs

W.L. MARTIN
HOME DESIGNS™

Price Code 13

plan name # CARTWRIGHT

plan number # #24048-9P

CARTWRIGHT

Columns visually separate the living room from the kitchen/dining room, which offer an island counter with snack bar and a view to the back.

- An uncluttered roofline helps to accentuate this home's understated exterior.

- A wrap-around porch leads inside where the living room is visible from the entry.

- The large size of the master bedroom makes it a great get-away spot where one can enjoy its abundant amenities.

- Two additional bedrooms share a compartmentalized bath with walk-in linen closet.

- The laundry room is smartly positioned near the secondary bedrooms and across from a full bath.

FINISHED SQ. FT.   1359

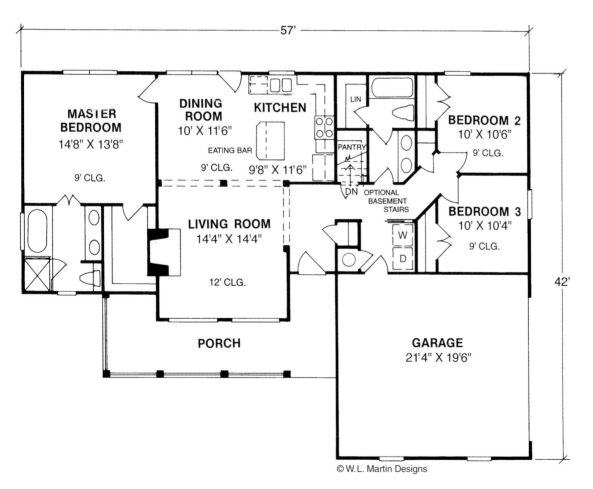

MASTER BEDROOM
14'8" X 13'8"

9' CLG.

DINING ROOM
10' X 11'6"

EATING BAR
9' CLG.

KITCHEN
9'8" X 11'6"

LIN

PANTRY

DN   OPTIONAL BASEMENT STAIRS

BEDROOM 2
10' X 10'6"
9' CLG.

LIVING ROOM
14'4" X 14'4"

12' CLG.

BEDROOM 3
10' X 10'4"
9' CLG.

W
D

PORCH

GARAGE
21'4" X 19'6"

57'

42'

First Floor

© W.L. Martin Designs

W.L. MARTIN
HOME DESIGNS™

Price Code 13

plan name **LINDALE**

plan number **#24035-9P**

A large living room has plenty of room to accommodate guests and features an 11-foot ceiling and a pair of double windows surrounding the fireplace.

- The use of brick on the front exterior of this home offers low maintenance.

- U-shaped counters in the kitchen create an efficient work area and offer service to the living room.

- The dining room features a double window and backyard access.

- The large master bedroom has an adjoining bath with walk-in closet and tub beneath a window.

- Bedroom 2 offers the visual appeal of an arched window and sloped ceiling.

FINISHED SQ. FT.   1395

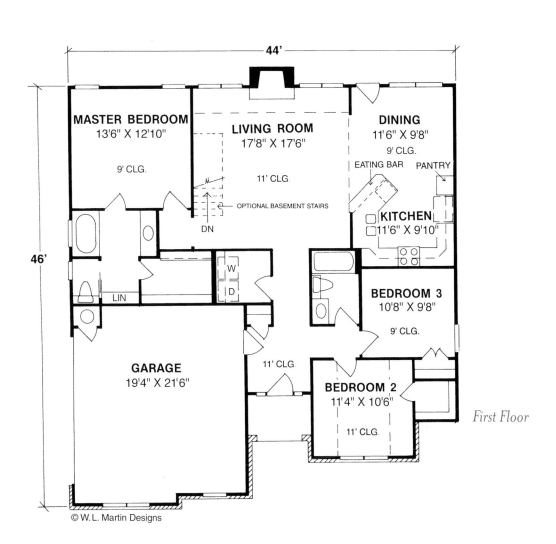

44'

46'

MASTER BEDROOM
13'6" X 12'10"

9' CLG.

LIVING ROOM
17'8" X 17'6"

11' CLG.

OPTIONAL BASEMENT STAIRS

DN

DINING
11'6" X 9'8"

9' CLG.

EATING BAR   PANTRY

KITCHEN
11'6" X 9'10"

W
D

LIN

BEDROOM 3
10'8" X 9'8"

9' CLG.

GARAGE
19'4" X 21'6"

11' CLG.

BEDROOM 2
11'4" X 10'6"

11' CLG.

First Floor

© W. L. Martin Designs

11

W.L. MARTIN
HOME DESIGNS™

Price Code 15

plan name **FELDON**

plan number **#24029-9P**

This home's front porch was meant to be used with its six-foot depth, 9-foot ceiling and large columns.

- Ten-foot ceilings add a sense of spaciousness to the living and dining rooms.

- Cabinets wrap around a central island with eating bar in the kitchen.

- Those in the master suite will enjoy its walk-in closet, soaking tub and double vanity.

- A compartmentalized bath serves the three additional bedrooms, allowing more than one to get ready.

- The garage offers a walk-in storage closet.

ORDER DIRECT
TOLL-FREE
(800) 947~7526
www.designbasics.com

FINISHED SQ. FT.   1539

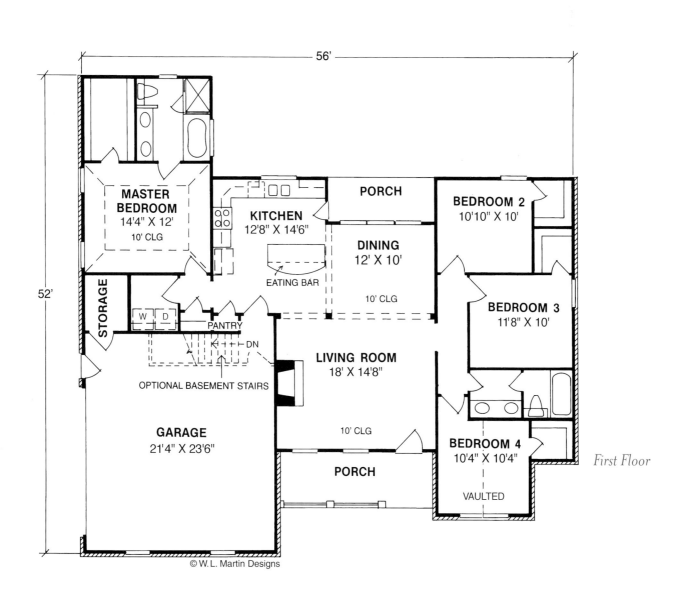

MASTER BEDROOM
14'4" X 12'
10' CLG

STORAGE

W   D

PANTRY

DN

OPTIONAL BASEMENT STAIRS

GARAGE
21'4" X 23'6"

KITCHEN
12'8" X 14'6"

EATING BAR

LIVING ROOM
18' X 14'8"

10' CLG

PORCH

DINING
12' X 10'
10' CLG

PORCH

BEDROOM 2
10'10" X 10'

BEDROOM 3
11'8" X 10'

BEDROOM 4
10'4" X 10'4"

VAULTED

First Floor

56'

52'

© W. L. Martin Designs

W.L. MARTIN

H O M E   D E S I G N S™

Price Code 15

plan name **CABRIE**

plan number **#24051-9P**

For added privacy, a wrap-around porch was positioned to the rear of this cottage-trimmed home.

- The kitchen's eating round is a perfect place to serve snacks or sit while conversing with the cook.

- The living room provides two window views, a corner fireplace and entertainment wall.

- Those in the dining room won't miss any activity in the living room and can access the rear porch.

- The master suite, with soaking bath and walk-in closet, has a direct connection to the laundry room.

- A work bench will be a welcome feature in the garage.

ORDER DIRECT
TOLL-FREE
(800) 947~7526
www.designbasics.com

FINISHED SQ. FT. **1541**

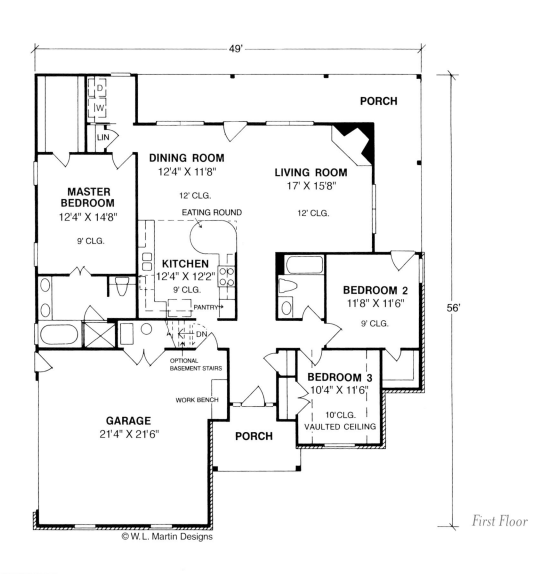

49'

PORCH

DINING ROOM
12'4" X 11'8"

LIVING ROOM
17' X 15'8"

12' CLG.

12' CLG.

D

W

LIN

MASTER
BEDROOM
12'4" X 14'8"

9' CLG.

EATING ROUND

KITCHEN
12'4" X 12'2"
9' CLG.

PANTRY

BEDROOM 2
11'8" X 11'6"

9' CLG.

DN

OPTIONAL
BASEMENT STAIRS

BEDROOM 3
10'4" X 11'6"

10' CLG.
VAULTED CEILING

WORK BENCH

GARAGE
21'4" X 21'6"

PORCH

56'

First Floor

© W. L. Martin Designs

W.L. MARTIN
HOME DESIGNS™

Price Code 16

plan name **MARGO**

plan number **#24017-9P**

MARGO

A single dormer and wrap-around porch define the appeal of this home's front elevation.

- Within steps of the dining room, the kitchen features a pantry and eating bar.

- Tucked between the breakfast nook and living room, a rear porch offers a place to get away.

- The master suite features French doors that open to a walk-in closet, double vanity and soaking tub.

- If the fourth bedroom isn't needed, it easily converts into a study.

- A walk-in storage closet in the garage is handy for placing tools and lawn equipment.

FINISHED SQ. FT.   1694

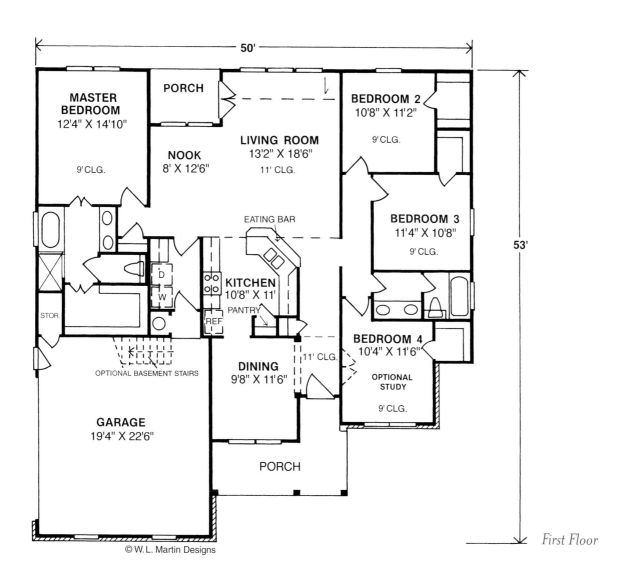

© W. L. Martin Designs

First Floor

W.L. MARTIN
HOME DESIGNS™

Price Code 17

plan name **TUXFORD**

plan number **#24003-9P**

From the entry, an archway leads into the breakfast nook, which provides a view to the front.

- Whatever the formal needs of the homeowner, the position of the dining room allows it to easily be used as a living room or home office.

- The large eating bar in the kitchen has room enough for the whole family to enjoy a casual meal.

- Privately located away from the other two bedrooms, the master suite features a corner garden tub with his-and-her vanities to each side.

- A row of windows frames a stunning view to the back in the family room with 11-foot ceiling.

- Two additional bedrooms share a full bath and linen closet.

CUSTOMIZE any home plan

FINISHED SQ. FT.   1762

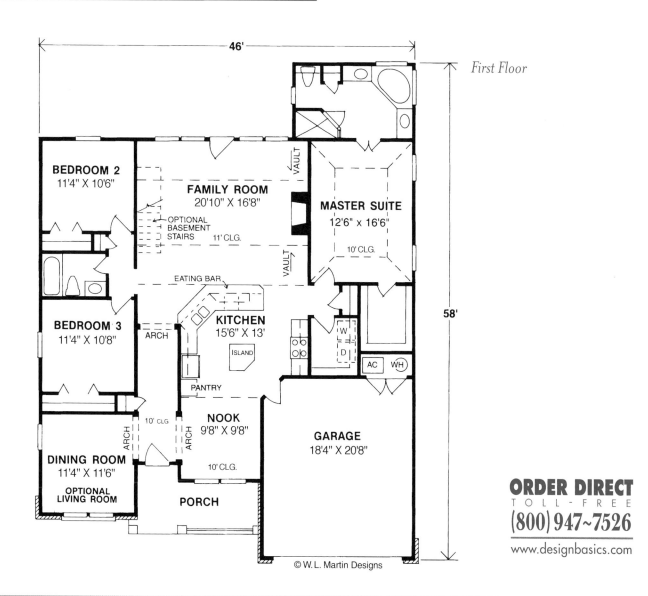

First Floor

BEDROOM 2
11'4" X 10'6"

FAMILY ROOM
20'10" X 16'8"
OPTIONAL BASEMENT STAIRS   11' CLG.

MASTER SUITE
12'6" x 16'6"
10' CLG.

VAULT

VAULT

EATING BAR

KITCHEN
15'6" X 13'
ISLAND

W
D

AC   WH

BEDROOM 3
11'4" X 10'8"

ARCH

PANTRY

10' CLG

ARCH

ARCH

NOOK
9'8" X 9'8"

GARAGE
18'4" X 20'8"

DINING ROOM
11'4" X 11'6"
OPTIONAL LIVING ROOM

10' CLG.

PORCH

46'

58'

© W. L. Martin Designs

19

W.L. MARTIN
HOME DESIGNS™

Price Code 17

plan name

WARREN

plan number **#24026-9P**

The foyer inside this home not only views the dining room, but also a built-in niche with barrel-vault archway above.

- The living room has a built-in TV unit beside a fireplace and is visually expanded by the inclusion of a triple rear window and 11-foot ceiling.

- A peninsula counter, pantry and eating bar are included in the kitchen.

- A pair of rooms with vaulted ceilings located to the rear of the home overlook a large porch, which is perfect for entertaining.

- A bayed sitting room, as well as a full bath with soaking tub and walk-in closet, highlight the master suite.

- Two additional bedrooms each have walk-in closets and share a full bath.

FINISHED SQ. FT.   1767

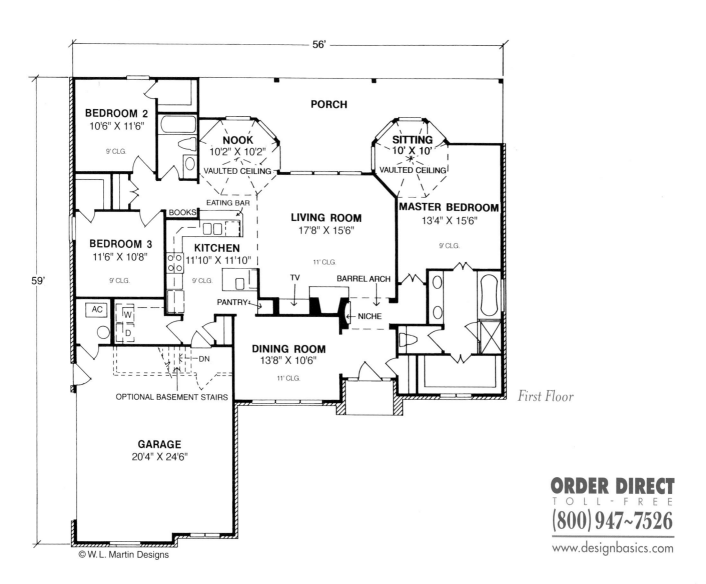

First Floor

© W. L. Martin Designs

W.L. MARTIN
HOME DESIGNS™

Price Code 18

plan name **HIGHLAND**

plan number **#24040-9P**

A vaulted ceiling soars to 11 feet in the master suite, which also features French doors that open to a soaking tub across from a double vanity.

- A combination of brick and siding comprise the elevation of this compact one-story home.

- To the left of the entry, the dining room is just steps from the kitchen.

- A walk-in pantry, circular counter and island offer convenience in the kitchen.

- The breakfast nook accesses a rear, covered porch.

- Bedroom 3 is made to feel spacious with a volume ceiling, while bedroom 2 offers a walk-in closet.

ORDER DIRECT
TOLL-FREE
(800) 947~7526
www.designbasics.com

FINISHED SQ. FT.   1810

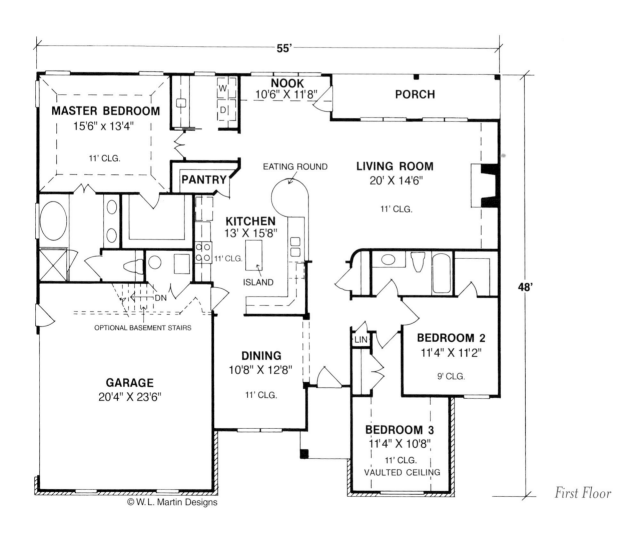

MASTER BEDROOM
15'6" x 13'4"
11' CLG.

NOOK
10'6" X 11'8"

PORCH

W
D

PANTRY

EATING ROUND

LIVING ROOM
20' X 14'6"
11' CLG.

KITCHEN
13' X 15'8"
11' CLG.

ISLAND

DN

OPTIONAL BASEMENT STAIRS

LIN

BEDROOM 2
11'4" X 11'2"
9' CLG.

GARAGE
20'4" X 23'6"

DINING
10'8" X 12'8"
11' CLG.

BEDROOM 3
11'4" X 10'8"
11' CLG.
VAULTED CEILING

55'

48'

First Floor

© W. L. Martin Designs

23

W.L. MARTIN
HOME DESIGNS™

Price Code 18

plan name **BROOKS**

plan number **#24020-9P**

Sturdy columns line the wrap-around front porch on this home and bring visual appeal to the front elevation.

- The kitchen features a walk-in pantry and eating bar that serves the breakfast nook and living room.

- French doors lead from the living room onto a rear, covered porch.

- An 11-foot ceiling towers over the master suite with separate walk-in closets, vanities and a soaking tub.

- Two additional bedrooms are located on the opposite end of the home from the master suite and feature walk-in closets.

- A closet in the garage provides a place for tool storage.

FINISHED SQ. FT.   1819

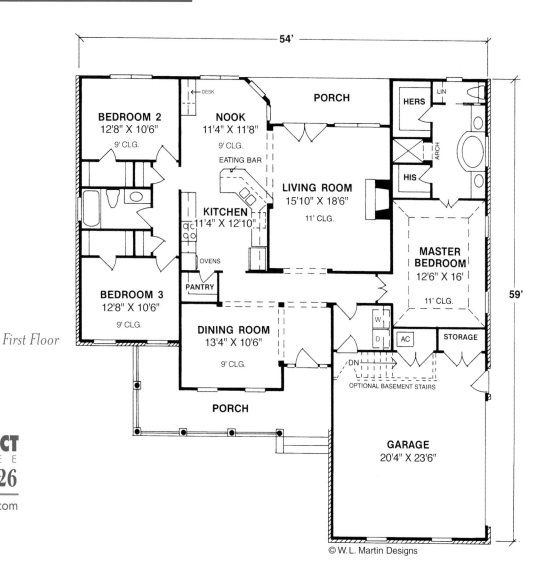

First Floor

BEDROOM 2
12'8" X 10'6"
9' CLG.

DESK

NOOK
11'4" X 11'8"
9' CLG.

EATING BAR

PORCH

HERS   LIN

ARCH

HIS

LIVING ROOM
15'10" X 18'6"
11' CLG.

KITCHEN
11'4" X 12'10"

OVENS

BEDROOM 3
12'8" X 10'6"
9' CLG.

PANTRY

MASTER BEDROOM
12'6" X 16'
11' CLG.

DINING ROOM
13'4" X 10'6"
9' CLG.

W
D   AC   STORAGE

DN

OPTIONAL BASEMENT STAIRS

PORCH

GARAGE
20'4" X 23'6"

54'

59'

© W. L. Martin Designs

W.L. MARTIN
HOME DESIGNS™

Price Code 18

plan name **LAROSE**

plan number **#24012-9P**

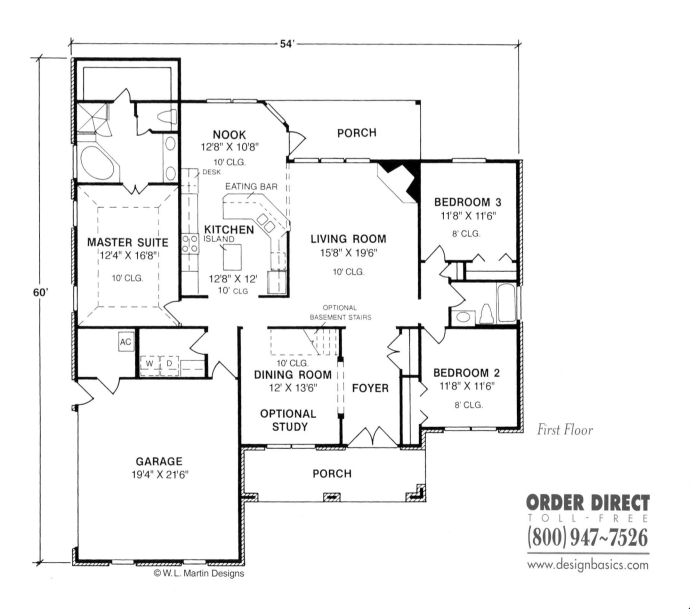

LAROSE

Afront porch with a pair of brick arches welcomes a bench for relaxing in the outdoors.

- The master suite is separated from two additional bedrooms and features an elegant corner shower, soaking tub and double vanity.
- Easily flexible as a study, the dining room is near the kitchen and features an elegant entry from the foyer.
- The best view may be available from a rear porch, accessible off the breakfast nook.
- An abundance of cabinets surround an island counter in the kitchen.
- A corner fireplace in the living room is visible from the kitchen and breakfast nook.

FINISHED SQ. FT.   1849

54'

60'

NOOK
12'8" X 10'8"
10' CLG.
DESK

PORCH

EATING BAR

KITCHEN
ISLAND
12'8" X 12'
10' CLG

MASTER SUITE
12'4" X 16'8"
10' CLG.

LIVING ROOM
15'8" X 19'6"
10' CLG.

BEDROOM 3
11'8" X 11'6"
8' CLG.

AC

W   D

OPTIONAL
BASEMENT STAIRS

10' CLG.

DINING ROOM
12' X 13'6"

FOYER

BEDROOM 2
11'8" X 11'6"
8' CLG.

**OPTIONAL
STUDY**

First Floor

GARAGE
19'4" X 21'6"

PORCH

© W. L. Martin Designs

W.L. MARTIN
HOME DESIGNS™

Price Code 19

plan name **BARBER**

plan number **#24021-9P**

Immediately inside this home, the foyer, dining and living rooms share the spaciousness of an 11-foot ceiling.

- A bayed sitting area provides a place to relax in the master bedroom.
- A double vanity, soaking tub and walk-in closet behind French doors comprise the master bath.
- Informal meals can be enjoyed at an eating bar in the kitchen or a bayed breakfast nook.
- Cabinets wrap around a central island for efficiency in the kitchen.
- A pair of double windows in the living room overlooks a rear porch.

ORDER DIRECT
TOLL-FREE
(800) 947~7526
www.designbasics.com

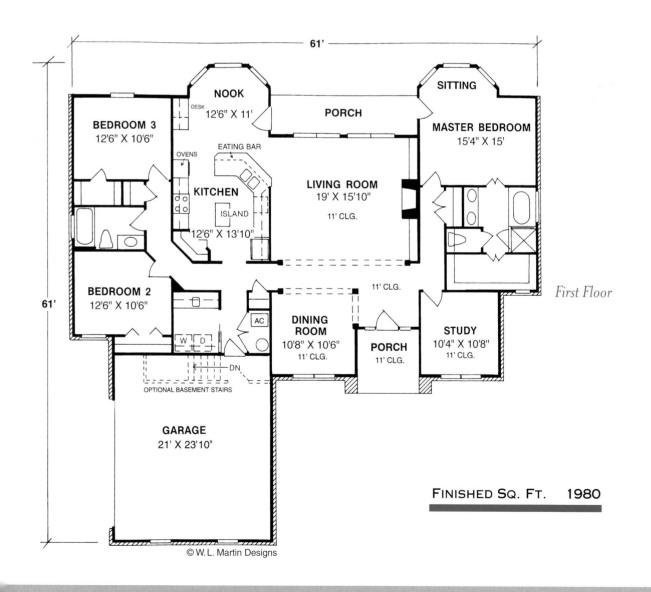

First Floor

FINISHED SQ. FT.   1980

© W. L. Martin Designs

Price Code 20

plan name **RICHDALE**

plan number **#24001-9P**

Guests entering this home can immediately enjoy the formal living and dining rooms with elegant columns, vaulted ceilings and dropped-soffit perimeters.

- At just 46 feet wide, this one-story home can accommodate a restrictive lot.

- A walk-through kitchen features a place for a table and includes a large eating bar.

- The family room's fireplace and French-door access to a back porch make it ideal to entertain informally.

- An indented, double-door entry reveals the master suite with vaulted ceiling, double vanity and corner garden tub.

- The laundry room is conveniently located near three additional bedrooms.

FINISHED SQ. FT.   2073

CUSTOMIZE
any home plan

ORDER DIRECT
TOLL-FREE
(800) 947~7526
www.designbasics.com

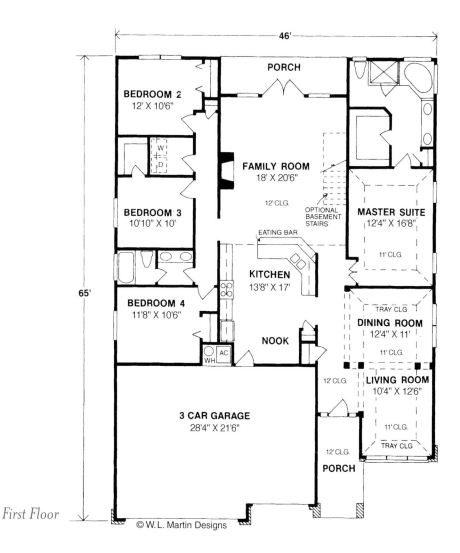

First Floor

© W.L. Martin Designs

W.L. MARTIN
HOME DESIGNS™

Price Code 21

plan name **CLARKSON**

plan number **#24038-9P**

This sprawling plantation style home is characterized by its extensive front porch and triple dormers resting on its gable roofline.

- A 12-foot ceiling in the entry steps down to 11 feet in the adjacent living and dining rooms.

- A built-in entertainment center in the family room offers a place for home electronics.

- A three-sided fireplace brings warmth to the kitchen, breakfast nook and family room.

- The master bedroom is positioned away from two additional bedrooms and has room for a pair of chairs beside its bayed window.

- Front and rear porches are great places to enjoy leisure time.

FINISHED SQ. FT.   2126

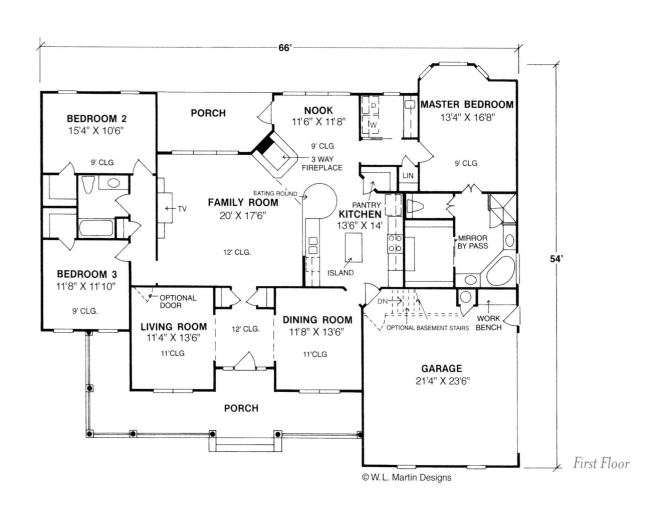

© W. L. Martin Designs

First Floor

W.L. MARTIN
HOME DESIGNS™

Price Code 21

plan name **OAKLAND**

plan number **#24027-9P**

Double doors hide the master suite which offers a sitting area and soaking tub for relaxing.

- A gable extension and columns form a wide stoop on this home's front porch.
- Symmetrical arches grant views into the study and dining room.
- The living room overlooks a rear porch and features a fireplace and 14-foot ceiling.
- A walk-in pantry and island with eating bar serve the kitchen.
- Three additional bedrooms are separated from the master suite and share a bath divided into compartments.

OAKLAND

ORDER DIRECT
TOLL-FREE
(800) 947~7526
www.designbasics.com

FINISHED SQ. FT.   2144

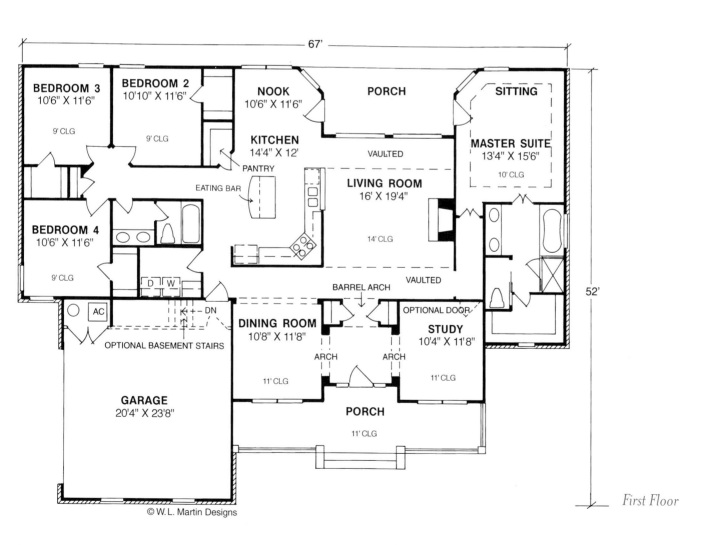

© W.L. Martin Designs

First Floor

W.L. MARTIN
HOME DESIGNS™

Price Code 22

plan name **HANSON**

plan number **#24002-9P**

This home's all brick facade showcases elegant windows that will be appreciated in the garage, dining room and study.

- Perfect for a home office, the study is located behind double doors and features an 11-foot ceiling.

- For everyday, meals can be enjoyed at the eating bar of the kitchen or in the sun-filled breakfast nook.

- A rear, covered porch extends the enjoyment of the living room.

- A double vanity, make-up counter and walk-in closet combine to create an optimal dressing area in the master bath.

- Three secondary bedrooms are separate from the master suite and share a compartmentalized bath.

ORIGINAL DRAFT
ALL PLANS HAVE BEEN REGISTERED
WITH THE U.S. COPYRIGHT OFFICE

FINISHED SQ. FT.   2250

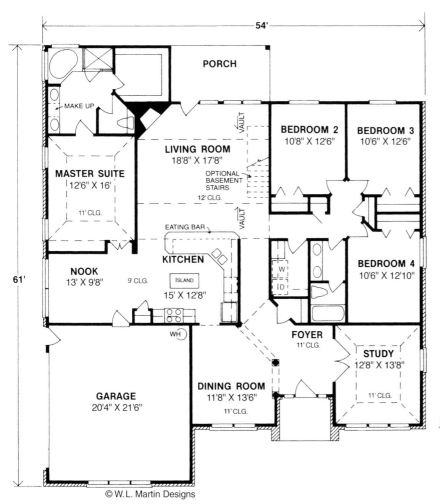

PORCH

MAKE UP

LIVING ROOM
18'8" X 17'8"

VAULT

BEDROOM 2
10'8" X 12'6"

BEDROOM 3
10'6" X 12'6"

MASTER SUITE
12'6" X 16'
11' CLG.

OPTIONAL BASEMENT STAIRS
12' CLG.

VAULT

EATING BAR

NOOK
13' X 9'8"
9' CLG.

KITCHEN
ISLAND
15' X 12'8"

W
D

BEDROOM 4
10'6" X 12'10"

WH

FOYER
11' CLG.

STUDY
12'8" X 13'8"
11' CLG.

GARAGE
20'4" X 21'6"

DINING ROOM
11'8" X 13'6"
11' CLG.

54'

61'

First Floor

© W. L. Martin Designs

ORDER DIRECT
TOLL-FREE
(800) 947~7526
www.designbasics.com

W.L. MARTIN
HOME DESIGNS™

Price Code 22

plan name **ROYSTON**

plan number **#24030-9P**

Inside this home, guests will enjoy a vaulted ceiling and fireplace in the living room, as well as its extension onto a rear porch.

• The study is perfect for time alone with its double doors and 11-foot ceiling.

• The kitchen is open to the living room and serves the breakfast area with an eating bar.

• French doors connect the master bedroom with its private bath, including a soaking tub across from a double vanity.

• Separated from the master suite, three additional bedrooms offer walk-in closets.

• A game room provides a second living space for children and guests.

ORDER DIRECT
TOLL-FREE
(800) 947~7526
www.designbasics.com

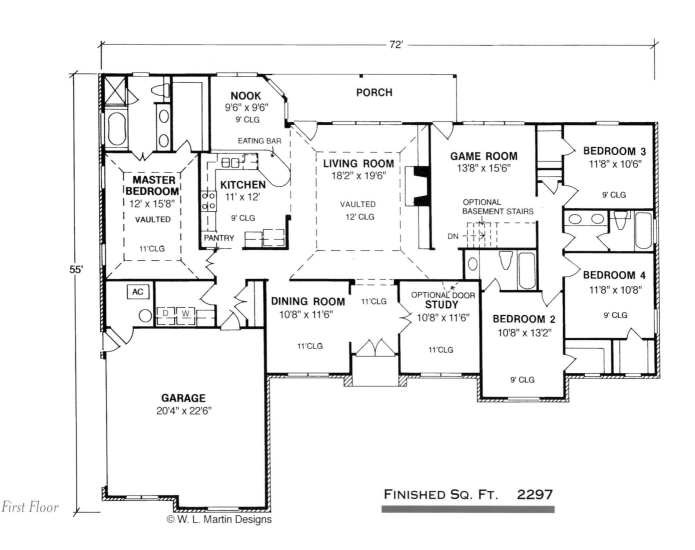

NOOK
9'6" x 9'6"
9' CLG

PORCH

EATING BAR

LIVING ROOM
18'2" x 19'6"

VAULTED
12' CLG

GAME ROOM
13'8" x 15'6"

BEDROOM 3
11'8" x 10'6"

9' CLG

MASTER BEDROOM
12' x 15'8"

VAULTED

11'CLG

KITCHEN
11' x 12'

9' CLG

PANTRY

OPTIONAL
BASEMENT STAIRS

DN

BEDROOM 4
11'8" x 10'8"

9' CLG

AC

D W

DINING ROOM
10'8" x 11'6"

11'CLG

11'CLG

OPTIONAL DOOR
STUDY
10'8" x 11'6"

11'CLG

BEDROOM 2
10'8" x 13'2"

9' CLG

GARAGE
20'4" x 22'6"

72'

55'

First Floor

© W. L. Martin Designs

FINISHED SQ. FT.   2297

W.L. MARTIN
HOME DESIGNS™

Price Code 23

plan name **MALONE**

plan number **#24033-9P**

A bayed turret is paired with a front porch framed by three arches on this elevation.

- The foyer includes a built-in niche and has a view of the living room and dining room through a series of arched openings.

- The kitchen has a beautiful display of cabinetry that includes a pantry, planning desk and a peninsula counter that accommodates an eating bar.

- A corner fireplace, 12-foot ceiling and French doors that open onto a rear porch complete the family room.

- Double doors reveal the master suite with two sets of French doors, one that opens to an adjoining bath and another onto a front porch.

- Three additional bedrooms are separated from the master suite and have walk-in closets.

FINISHED SQ. FT. 2334

First Floor

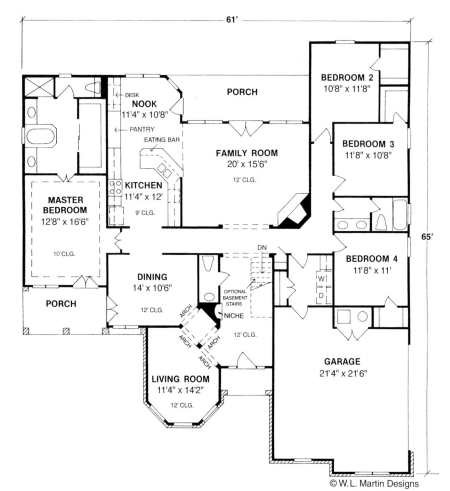

© W. L. Martin Designs

ORDER DIRECT
TOLL-FREE
(800) 947~7526
www.designbasics.com

W.L. MARTIN
HOME DESIGNS™

Price Code 24

plan name **PEARL**

plan number **#24014-9P**

Both the dining room and study in this home offer nearly floor-to-ceiling windows viewing the front.

- Double doors open to a study neatly tucked in the front of this home.

- The open arrangement of the kitchen, breakfast nook and family room will create a comfortable place to relax.

- A rear porch adjoins the living areas of the home, making it a great spot for entertaining in fair weather.

- Corner bayed windows provide a rear view in the master bedroom.

- Three additional bedrooms are separate from the master suite and feature walk-in closets.

(800) 947~

www.designbasics.com

FINISHED SQ. FT.   2451

First Floor

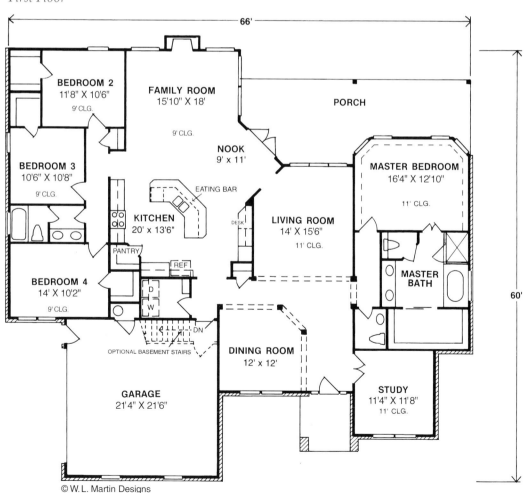

© W. L. Martin Designs

I like placing the master suite on the main level because buyers get the look of a two-story home, with the convenience of a one-story.

It is one of the most cost-effective designs there is to build because you can utilize that attic space for additional bedrooms, play rooms or living space. When I'm designing, I try to look at how the rooflines come together so I can utilize as much of that upper-level attic space as I can. Being able to use the space in that way creates a nice exterior and gives a larger look to the home.

—W.L. Martin

Plan #	Plan Name	Sq. Ft.	Page #
24034	Claiborne	1896	46-47
24016	Barons	1897	48-49
24008	Belany	1955	50-51
24037	Simons	2086	52-53
24039	Thayer	2101	54-55
24004	Bardel	2248	56-57
24025	Glenwood	2297	58-59
24028	Butler	2384	60-61
24009	Wainright	2420	62-63
24031	Dellwood	2525	64-65
24022	Formosa	2575	66-67
24018	Glenrock	2606	68-69
24010	Lamar	2642	70-71
24011	Oliver	2688	72-73
24015	Fairview	2755	74-75
24006	Fenwick	2837	76-77
24036	Bartow	2874	78-79
24024	Pasadena	2878	80-81
24032	Vernon	2935	82-83
24013	Salina	2953	84-85
24007	Pembrook	2978	86-87
24019	Belmont	3844	88-89
24041	Lagoda	3914	90-91

W.L. MARTIN
HOME DESIGNS™

Price Code 18

plan name # CLAIBORNE

plan number # #24034-9P

CLAIBORNE

The exterior of this home displays decorative shutters and a front porch with large, round columns.

- The dining room is visible from the foyer and views the front through a triple window.

- The kitchen is open on two ends and positioned adjacent to the formal and informal eating areas.

- A rear porch is meant to relax upon and take in the rear view.

- A window seat is perfect to accompany a dual-sink vanity and soaking tub in the master bath.

- The upper level of this home is accessed from a rear staircase, which leads to a game room overlooking the living room.

FIRST FLOOR	1334
SECOND FLOOR	562
TOTAL SQ. FT.	1896

Second Floor

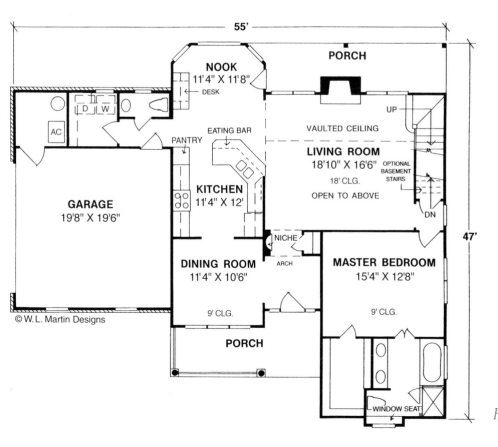

© W.L. Martin Designs

First Floor

ORDER DIRECT
TOLL-FREE
(800) 947~7526
www.designbasics.com

47

W.L. MARTIN
HOME DESIGNS™

Price Code 18

plan name **BARONS**

plan number **#24016-9P**

The master suite is near the laundry room and features a walk-in closet, soaking tub, separate shower and dual-sink vanity.

- Just beyond the entry in this home, a ceiling soars two stories in the family room.

- A vaulted ceiling emphasizes the dining room's front window.

- Adjoining the kitchen are a butler's pantry and serving counter.

- An upper-level attic offers a place for storage within this home.

- Two additional bedrooms on the second level share a full bath.

FIRST FLOOR	1448
SECOND FLOOR	449
TOTAL SQ. FT.	1897

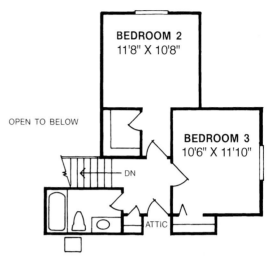

Second Floor

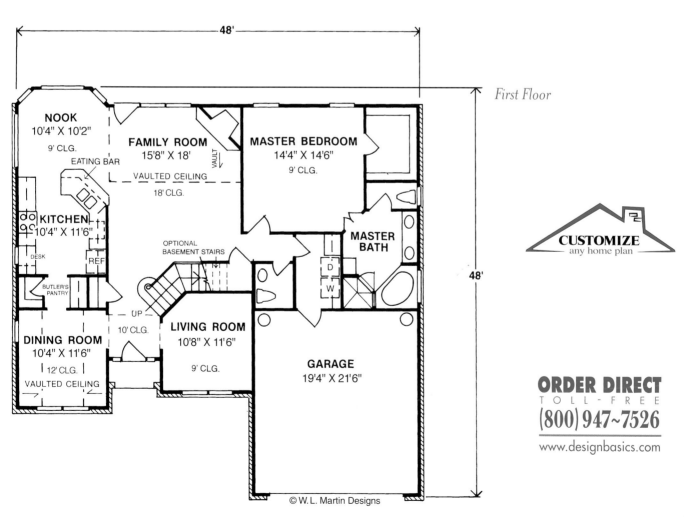

First Floor

CUSTOMIZE
any home plan

ORDER DIRECT
TOLL-FREE
(800) 947~7526
www.designbasics.com

© W. L. Martin Designs

49

W.L. MARTIN
HOME DESIGNS™

Price Code 19

plan name **BELANY**

plan number **#24008-9P**

BELANY

A double gable creates a spotlight for double-hung windows trimmed with soldier coursing and a decorative eave.

- A charming archway with built-in niches leads to the formal dining room that can also be converted into a study.

- A trio of windows brightens the breakfast nook which includes the option of a built-in desk.

- His-and-her vanities are across from a soaking tub and separate shower in the master bath.

- Secluded on the main floor, the master bedroom is highlighted with a vaulted ceiling.

- Additional space off the corridor provides an opportunity to expand the second level.

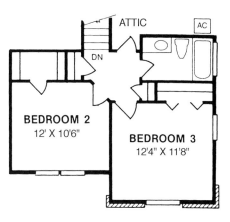

Second Floor

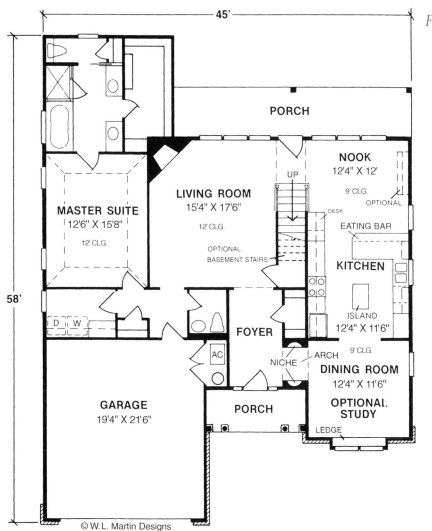

First Floor

FIRST FLOOR	1500
SECOND FLOOR	455
TOTAL SQ. FT.	1955

© W. L. Martin Designs

W.L. MARTIN
HOME DESIGNS™

Price Code 20

plan name **SIMONS**

plan number **#24037-9P**

Attractive windows mask this home's side-load garage from view of the street.

- This home's front porch welcomes a swing or pair of chairs for relaxing.
- A walk-in pantry is ideal for food and appliance storage in the kitchen.
- A built-in TV cabinet is located next to a fireplace in the living room.
- The master suite features a bayed sitting area and walk-in closet with built-in dresser.
- Guests will enjoy the private bath in bedroom 2 on the upper level.

FIRST FLOOR	1383
SECOND FLOOR	703
TOTAL SQ. FT.	2086

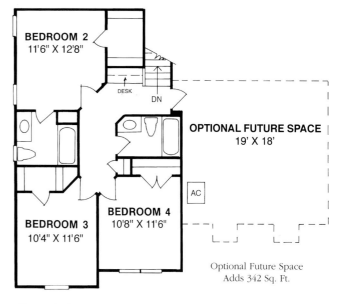

Optional Future Space
Adds 342 Sq. Ft.

Second Floor

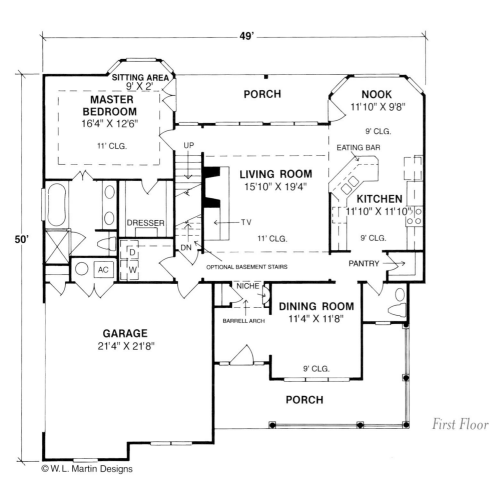

First Floor

ORDER DIRECT
TOLL-FREE
(800) 947~7526
www.designbasics.com

© W. L. Martin Designs

W.L. MARTIN
HOME DESIGNS™

Price Code 21

plan name # THAYER

plan number # #24039-9P

This home's traditional styling is not marred by the garage, which is placed to the rear.

- Those who work at home will appreciate the study, located just inside the entry.

- A large kitchen shares space with a nook and includes an island, pantry and access to a side porch.

- A bayed sitting room in the master suite allows one to take advantage of the rear view and a covered porch.

- Both upper-level bedrooms have walk-in closets and adjoin a computer center.

- Additional storage space can be added through attic space accessible on the upper level.

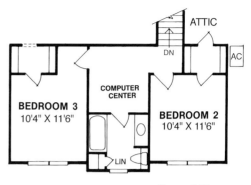

Second Floor

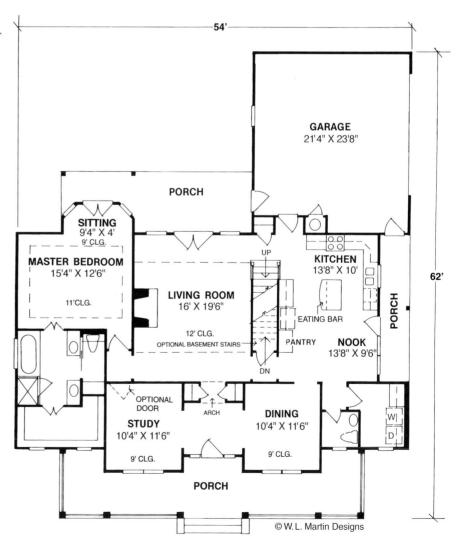

First Floor

FIRST FLOOR	1612
SECOND FLOOR	489
TOTAL SQ. FT.	2101

ORDER DIRECT
T O L L - F R E E
(800) 947~7526
www.designbasics.com

© W. L. Martin Designs

W.L. MARTIN
HOME DESIGNS™

Price Code 22

plan name **BARDEL**

plan number **#24004-9P**

A large walk-in closet, twin-sink vanity and corner garden tub make the master suite a luxurious retreat.

- A shed roof and vertical siding give this home it's cottage feel.

- A butler's pantry conveniently adjoins the dining room with vaulted ceiling.

- In the kitchen, an angled snack bar connects the family room and breakfast nook.

- All three second-floor bedrooms include walk-in closets.

- Attic space off the bath offers the option of adding storage on the second level.

FIRST FLOOR	1568
SECOND FLOOR	680
TOTAL SQ. FT.	2248

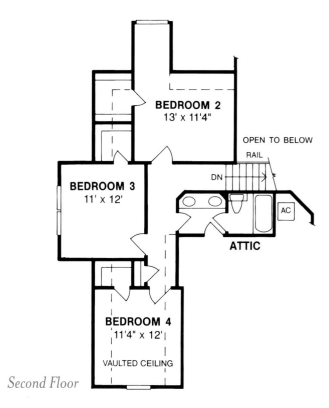

Second Floor

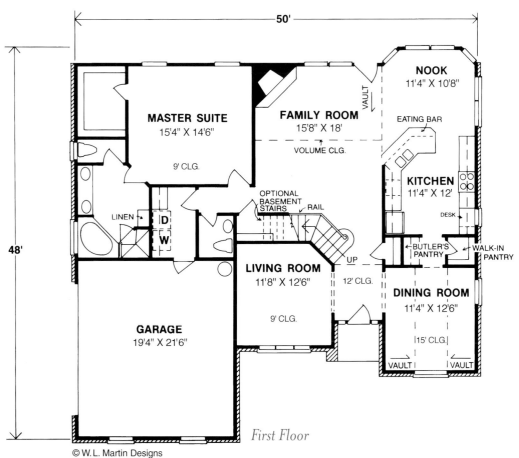

First Floor

© W.L. Martin Designs

W.L. MARTIN
HOME DESIGNS™

Price Code 22

plan name # GLENWOOD

plan number **#24025-9P**

Double doors shield the master suite from view. The master bath features a soaking tub under windows, double vanity with appliance garage and walk-in closet.

- Columns define the kitchen with pantry, corner stove and island counter with eating bar.

- The living room includes a fireplace and adjoins a rear porch.

- A front porch extending the length of this elevation beckons all to relax outdoors.

- The garage is located to the rear of the home and has a streamlined path to the utility area and kitchen.

- Dormers offer a quaint place to read in two upper-level bedrooms.

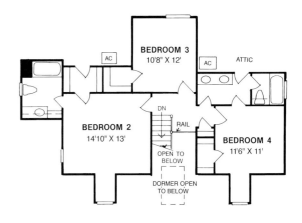

Second Floor

First Floor

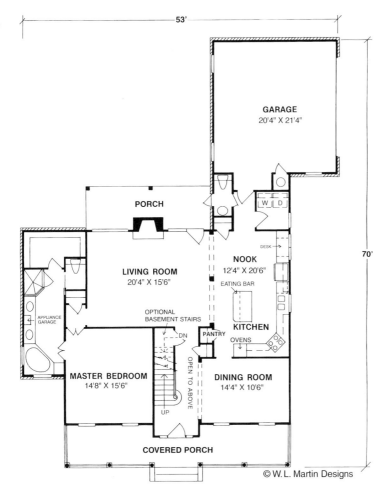

© W. L. Martin Designs

FIRST FLOOR	1492
SECOND FLOOR	805
TOTAL SQ. FT.	**2297**

ORDER DIRECT
TOLL-FREE
(800) 947~7526
www.designbasics.com

W.L. MARTIN
HOME DESIGNS™

Price Code 23

plan name # BUTLER

plan number # #24028-9P

A wrap-around porch leads inside this home, where the dining room is open.

- The living room can be viewed from an upper-level balcony and features a fireplace.

- The study, located behind double doors, makes an ideal office for those who work at home.

- The kitchen is equipped with an appliance garage, pantry and eating bar.

- A rear staircase allows those in the family area of the home to quickly access the upper level.

- An unfinished bonus room offers plenty of space for storage on the second level.

FIRST FLOOR	1616
SECOND FLOOR	768
TOTAL SQ. FT.	2384

Second Floor

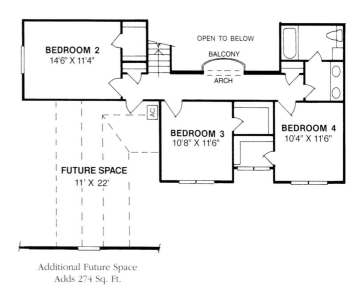

Additional Future Space
Adds 274 Sq. Ft.

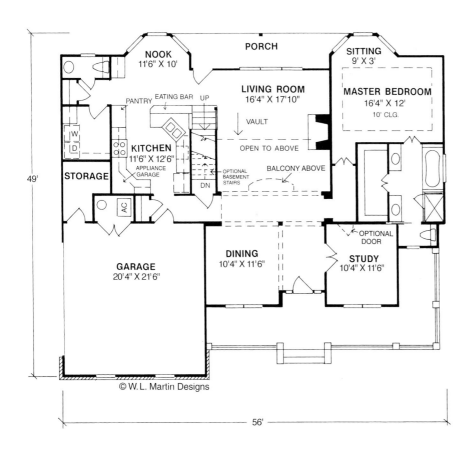

© W.L. Martin Designs

First Floor

CUSTOMIZE
any home plan

ORDER DIRECT
TOLL-FREE
(800) 947~7526
www.designbasics.com

W.L. MARTIN
HOME DESIGNS™

Price Code 24

plan name **WAINRIGHT**

plan number **#24009-9P**

In this design, an expansive living room welcomes family and friends and features a warm fireplace and view to the back.

- Just off the foyer, the dining room features an angled entry and 11-foot ceiling.

- A truly secluded master suite offers a private porch to get away to and a luxurious bath with dual-sink vanity, opulent soaking tub and large walk-in closet.

- Perfect for homework or household planning, a second-level loft provides plenty of room for the family computer.

- A child's play area could be created in an optional third-level game room.

- A window seat makes a picturesque place to read in bedroom 2.

Second Floor

FIRST FLOOR	1601
SECOND FLOOR	819
TOTAL SQ. FT.	2420

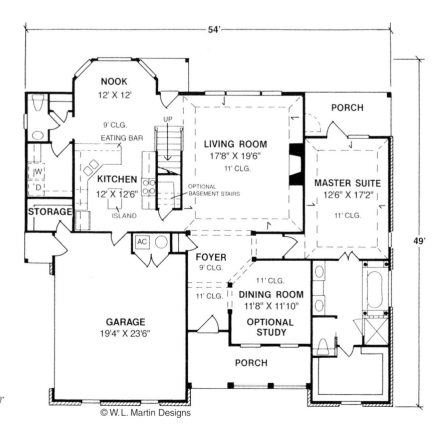

First Floor

© W. L. Martin Designs

ORDER DIRECT
TOLL-FREE
(800) 947~7526
www.designbasics.com

W.L. MARTIN
HOME DESIGNS™

Price Code 25

plan name # DELLWOOD

plan number **#24031-9P**

With its efficient roofline and foundation, this design is an economical choice to build.

- The front porch leads inside, where the living and dining rooms flank the entry.

- An 18-foot ceiling tops the family room featuring a fireplace and built-ins.

- The kitchen easily serves guests with an eating bar and butler's pantry.

- With a snack counter and sink, the game room is a great place for kids to entertain their friends.

- A walk-in closet and bath with dual-sink vanity and whirlpool tub serve the master bedroom.

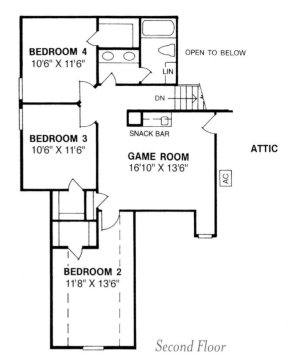

Second Floor

First Floor

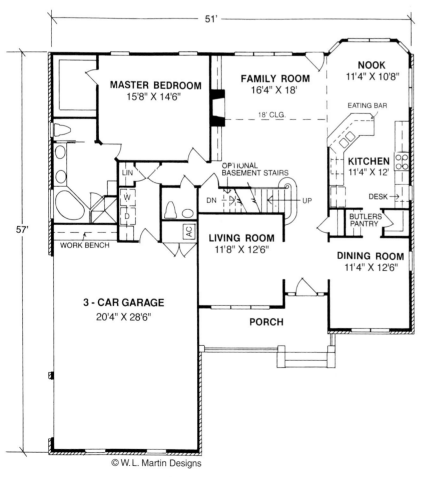

© W. L. Martin Designs

FIRST FLOOR	1604
SECOND FLOOR	921
TOTAL SQ. FT.	2525

W.L. MARTIN
HOME DESIGNS™

Price Code 25

plan name **FORMOSA**

plan number **#24022-9P**

This appealing elevation hides the prominence of its three-car garage beneath a double gable on the upper level.

- With location to the front of the home, the study is a great place for quiet relaxation.

- An island counter with cooktop and walk-in pantry make work easy in the kitchen.

- An 18-foot ceiling towers above a fireplace in the living room.

- A rear staircase in the living room accesses the second level with three bedrooms and a game room.

- French doors connect the master suite with a covered porch.

Second Floor

First Floor

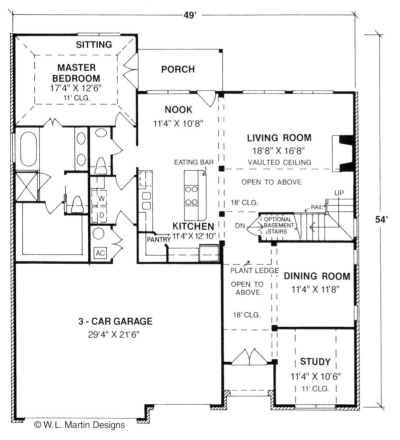

© W. L. Martin Designs

FIRST FLOOR	1623
SECOND FLOOR	952
TOTAL SQ. FT.	2575

ORDER DIRECT
TOLL-FREE
(800) 947~7526
www.designbasics.com

W.L. MARTIN
HOME DESIGNS™

Price Code 26

plan name **GLENROCK**

plan number **#24018-9P**

Double gables carry the eye from this home's entry to it's functional, three-car garage.

- Adjacent to the foyer, the study can combine with the dining room when entertaining or serve as its own private retreat.

- The living room has an optional fireplace and is open to the kitchen and breakfast nook.

- French doors open to a walk-in closet in the master bath.

- A game room can be finished on the upper level to accompany three additional bedrooms.

- Extra counter space is handy for working in the laundry room.

Second Floor

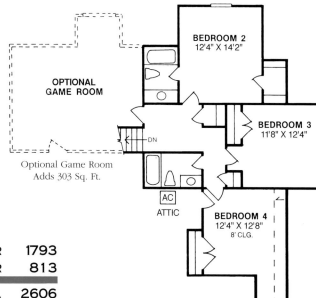

Optional Game Room
Adds 303 Sq. Ft.

FIRST FLOOR	1793
SECOND FLOOR	813
TOTAL SQ. FT.	2606

First Floor

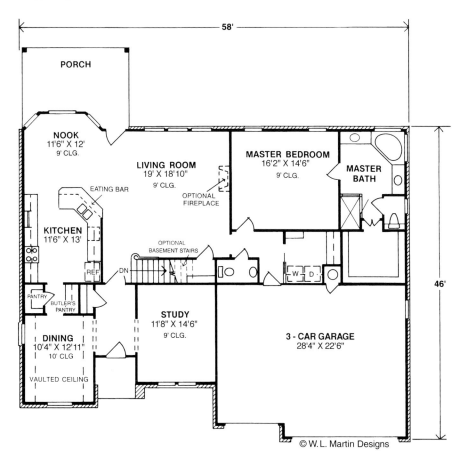

© W. L. Martin Designs

ORDER DIRECT
T O L L - F R E E
(800) 947~7526
www.designbasics.com

W.L. MARTIN
HOME DESIGNS™

Price Code 26

plan name **LAMAR**

plan number **#24010-9P**

A single dormer adds charm to this home's front elevation, when paired with a hip roofline and windows trimmed with shutters.

- The kitchen's eating bar is open to the family room, making it convenient to serve snacks or buffet-style meals.

- A walk-in closet offers storage space to bedroom 2, while its window seat adds charm.

- The second level can easily be expanded by finishing an optional game room.

- The family room feels additional spaciousness from an 11-foot vaulted ceiling and light from four rear windows.

- The master suite is removed from main-level activity and is close to the laundry room.

Optional Game Room
Adds 219 Sq. Ft.

OPTIONAL GAME ROOM

BEDROOM 3
13'10" X 11'4"

BEDROOM 2
11'8" X 12'8"

DN
UP

AC

7'8" X 5'
WINDOW SEAT

BEDROOM 4
10'4" X 12'8"

Second Floor

FIRST FLOOR	1730
SECOND FLOOR	912
TOTAL SQ. FT.	2642

First Floor

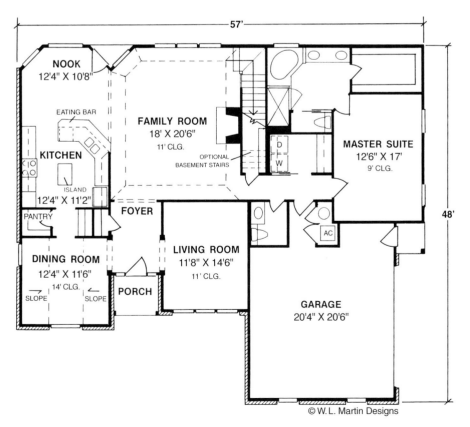

NOOK
12'4" X 10'8"

EATING BAR

FAMILY ROOM
18' X 20'6"
11' CLG.

OPTIONAL
BASEMENT STAIRS

MASTER SUITE
12'6" X 17'
9' CLG.

KITCHEN
ISLAND
12'4" X 11'2"

PANTRY

FOYER

D
W

AC

DINING ROOM
12'4" X 11'6"
14' CLG.
SLOPE   SLOPE

PORCH

LIVING ROOM
11'8" X 14'6"
11' CLG.

GARAGE
20'4" X 20'6"

57'

48'

© W. L. Martin Designs

ORDER DIRECT
TOLL-FREE
(800) 947~7526
www.designbasics.com

W.L. MARTIN
HOME DESIGNS™

Price Code 26

plan name **OLIVER**

plan number **#24011-9P**

The strong traditional lines and front porch on this home's facade will make it a welcome addition to any neighborhood.

- The flexible dining room/study, just inside the entry, makes this home adaptable to a variety of lifestyles.

- An island counter is centrally located in the kitchen to shorten steps from the stove and sink.

- A bright breakfast nook is flooded with natural light through bayed windows.

- An 11-foot ceiling towers over the master bedroom with adjoining full bath and walk-in closet.

- Perfect for children, a large play room can be easily accessed by three upper-level bedrooms.

FIRST FLOOR	1650
SECOND FLOOR	1038
TOTAL SQ. FT.	2688

Second Floor

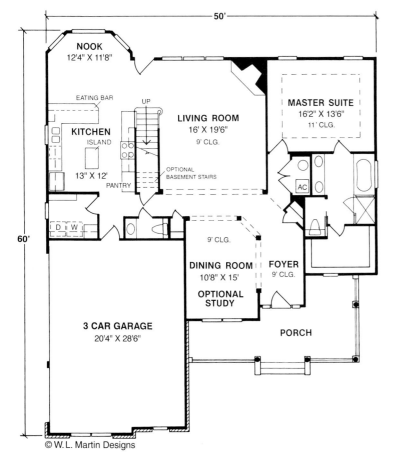

First Floor

© W. L. Martin Designs

ORDER DIRECT
TOLL-FREE
(800) 947~7526
www.designbasics.com

W.L. MARTIN
HOME DESIGNS™

Price Code 27

plan name **FAIRVIEW**

plan number **#24015-9P**

Batten-board shutters give a casual treatment to the windows on this all-brick front elevation.

- A vaulted ceiling reaches 12 feet in height in the study.

- A centrally-located kitchen easily serves the breakfast nook, dining room and family room.

- Positioned to the rear of the home, the master suite enjoys a walk-in closet, corner soaking tub, dual-sink vanity and trayed ceiling.

- Three bedrooms on the upper-level have access to a game room.

- A tandem, three-car garage allows this home to be useable on a restrictive lot.

Second Floor

First Floor

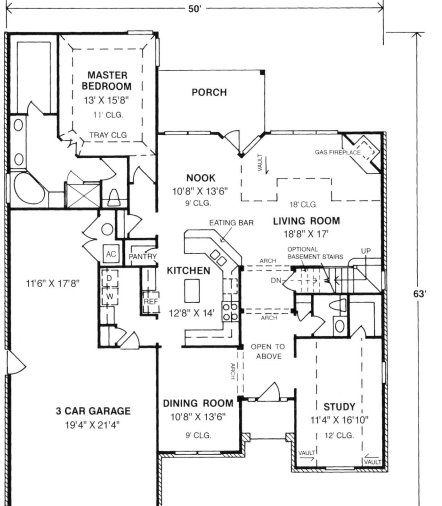

© W. L. Martin Designs

FIRST FLOOR	1830
SECOND FLOOR	925
TOTAL SQ. FT.	2755

ORDER DIRECT
TOLL-FREE
(800) 947~7526
www.designbasics.com

W.L. MARTIN
HOME DESIGNS™

Price Code 28

plan name **FENWICK**

plan number **#24006-9P**

I n this design, an open kitchen, family room and breakfast area will make it easy for a family to be together while involved in separate activities.

- A built-in china cabinet brings a nice touch to the formal dining room.

- The master suite offers the convenience of a large walk-in closet, linen cabinet, twin-lav vanity and corner tub.

- Bedroom 2 makes the perfect guest or in-law suite with its own bath and walk-in closet.

- A rear porch will make it easy to enjoy the outdoors and take in the rear view.

- A second-level game room provides a place for children to play or study.

Second Floor

BEDROOM 3
11'4" X 12'

OPEN TO BELOW

DN

OPEN TO BELOW

BEDROOM 4
12'8" X 12'4"

GAME ROOM
11'4" X 10'8"

AC

ATTIC

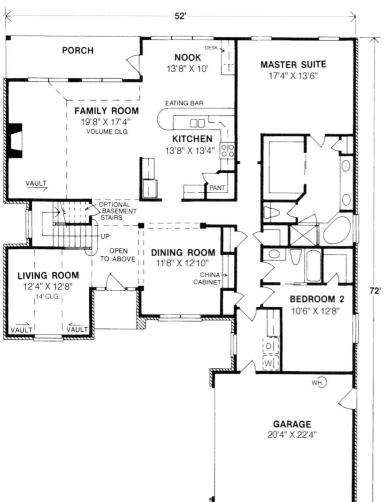

52'

PORCH

NOOK
13'8" X 10'

DESK

MASTER SUITE
17'4" X 13'6"

FAMILY ROOM
19'8" X 17'4"
VOLUME CLG

EATING BAR

KITCHEN
13'8" X 13'4"

VAULT

PANT.

OPTIONAL BASEMENT STAIRS

UP

OPEN TO ABOVE

DINING ROOM
11'8" X 12'10"

CHINA CABINET

LIVING ROOM
12'4" X 12'8"
14' CLG.

VAULT   VAULT

BEDROOM 2
10'6" X 12'8"

D
W

72'

WH

GARAGE
20'4" X 22'4"

First Floor

© W. L. Martin Designs

FIRST FLOOR	2167
SECOND FLOOR	670
TOTAL SQ. FT.	2837

ORDER DIRECT
TOLL-FREE
(800) 947~7526
www.designbasics.com

W.L. MARTIN
HOME DESIGNS™

Price Code 28

plan name **BARTOW**

plan number **#24036-9P**

The tall covered stoop on this design frames an arched transom above French doors leading inside.

- The dining room is open to a living room and is joined by a butler's pantry.

- The kitchen includes a walk-in pantry and an island with two-person eating bar.

- French doors in the breakfast area open to a rear porch.

- An upper-level game room accompanies three bedrooms and includes a dormer with rear view and a large closet.

- Bayed windows in the master bedroom create room for a sitting area.

Second Floor

FIRST FLOOR	1803
SECOND FLOOR	1071
TOTAL SQ. FT.	2874

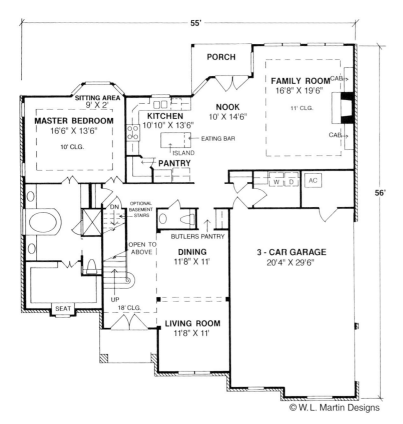

First Floor

© W. L. Martin Designs

ORDER DIRECT
TOLL-FREE
(800) 947~7526
www.designbasics.com

W.L. MARTIN
Home Designs™

Price Code 28

plan name **PASADENA**

plan number **#24024-9P**

The predominantly brick elevation on this home offers low maintenance for homeowners.

- The two-story foyer views an upper-level catwalk and barrel-vault ceiling with built-in niches.

- A corner fireplace accents the living room with French doors that extend to a rear, covered porch.

- A large eating bar and bayed breakfast nook provide places to eat an informal meal.

- Built-in bookshelves provide a place for books and toy storage in the upper-level game room.

- All three upper-level bedrooms feature walk-in closets and share two full baths.

Second Floor

First Floor

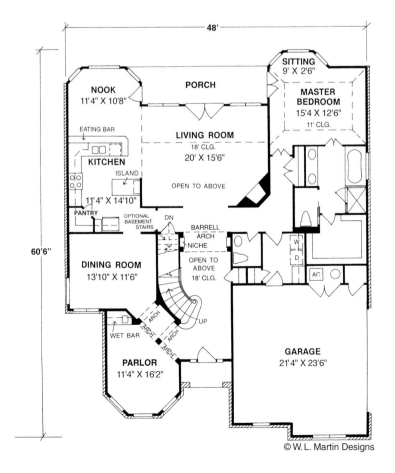

© W. L. Martin Designs

FIRST FLOOR	1850
SECOND FLOOR	1028
TOTAL SQ. FT.	2878

W.L. MARTIN
HOME DESIGNS™

Price Code 29

plan name **VERNON**

plan number **#24032-9P**

VERNON

The kicked eaves on this home's roofline are an interesting twist on the strictly traditional exterior.

- A study is enclosed behind double doors and has the option of a second entry near the master suite.

- Columns help define the living room with fireplace and a row of double windows to the rear.

- An island counter is centrally located in the kitchen to cut down on steps between food preparation areas.

- Two porches allow a private getaway.

- A bayed sitting area in the master suite provides a place to unwind at the end of the day.

FIRST FLOOR	1863
SECOND FLOOR	1072
TOTAL SQ. FT.	2935

Second Floor

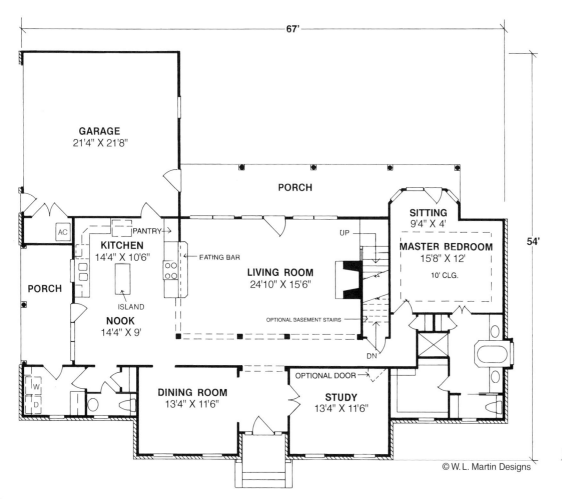

First Floor

© W.L. Martin Designs

ORDER DIRECT
TOLL-FREE
(800) 947~7526
www.designbasics.com

W.L. MARTIN
HOME DESIGNS™

Price Code 29

plan name **SALINA**

plan number **#24013-9P**

French doors reveal a grand foyer and offer the visual excitement of a curving stairway and built-in niche.

- A trio of archways leads to the living room with sloped ceiling and corner fireplace between two walls of windows.

- A wrap-around porch extends the rear of the home and makes a great place to entertain outdoors.

- Bedroom 2 makes an ideal guest suite with its walk-in closet and full bath.

- A large bonus room can be added to the second level.

- Bedrooms 3 and 4 share a Hollywood bath with double vanity.

FIRST FLOOR	2046
SECOND FLOOR	907
TOTAL SQ. FT.	2953

Second Floor

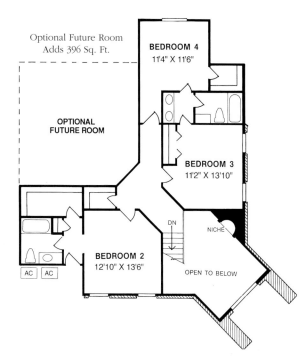

First Floor

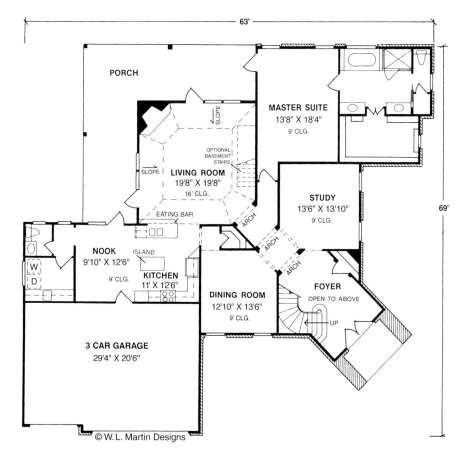

© W. L. Martin Designs

ORDER DIRECT
TOLL - FREE
(800) 947~7526
www.designbasics.com

W.L. MARTIN
HOME DESIGNS™

Price Code 29

plan name **PEMBROOK**

plan number **#24007-9P**

A second-floor walkway is visible inside this home's two-story entry and family room.

- A stucco and brick combination on the exterior adds to this home's stately appeal.

- Two walls of windows brighten a retreat in the master suite, providing a place for reading or quiet relaxation.

- Whether studying or playing games, the children will enjoy the open study and play room on the second level.

- A back porch is a wonderful place to enjoy the outdoors while entertaining.

- Storage space is provided in the garage for lawn and garden equipment.

FIRST FLOOR	2101
SECOND FLOOR	877
TOTAL SQ. FT.	2978

Second Floor

First Floor

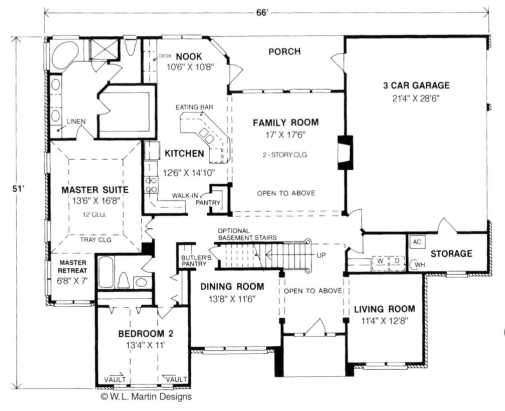

© W. L. Martin Designs

W.L. MARTIN

HOME DESIGNS™

Price Code 38

plan name **BELMONT**

plan number **#24019-9P**

BELMONT

The brick tower on this home's front elevation encloses a main-level study with fireplace and a second-level bedroom with walk-in closet.

- The large dining room has plenty of space to seat guests and is near a serving counter.

- An arched opening leads to the living room with view past a rear porch.

- The master suite includes an octagonal-shape sitting area, two walk-in closets and separate vanities.

- A bayed breakfast nook enjoys a sloped ceiling and plenty of natural light.

- A second-level game room offers a place for children to play and do schoolwork.

FIRST FLOOR	2496
SECOND FLOOR	1348
TOTAL SQ. FT.	3844

Second Floor

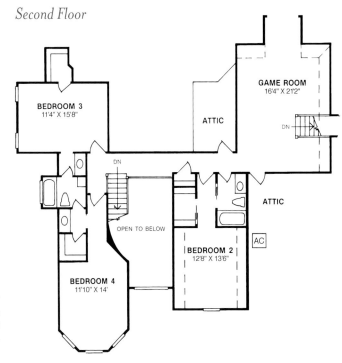

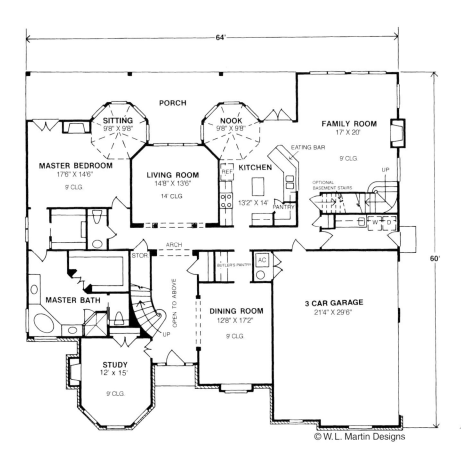

First Floor

© W. L. Martin Designs

ORDER DIRECT
TOLL-FREE
(800) 947~7526
www.designbasics.com

89

W.L. MARTIN
HOME DESIGNS™

Price Code 39

plan name **LAGODA**

plan number **#24041-9P**

The casual atmosphere extended by this home's exterior is carried on inside where spacious living areas comfortably entertain.

- To either side of the entry, columns form the living and dining rooms.

- A massive walk-in pantry in the kitchen has more than enough room for food and small appliance storage.

- Double doors open to the master bedroom, featuring a bayed sitting area with access to a rear porch.

- Columns frame the soaking tub across from a double vanity in the master bath.

- The second-level game room features built-ins for computer and electronic equipment.

Second Floor

FIRST FLOOR	2472
SECOND FLOOR	1442
TOTAL SQ. FT.	**3914**

First Floor

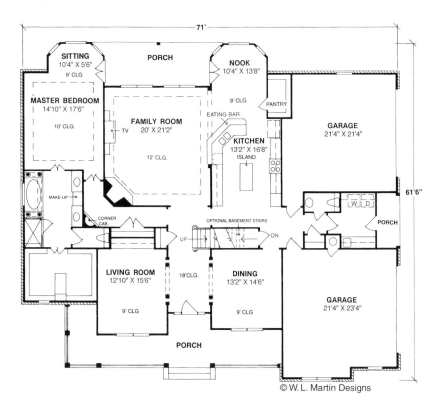

© W. L. Martin Designs

CUSTOMIZE
any home plan

ORDER DIRECT
TOLL-FREE
(800) 947~7526

www.designbasics.com

When I'm designing two-story homes, I try to provide as much separation for the bedrooms as I can. I do that by creating two separate hallways to access the master suite and the other bedrooms. I feel that when the master suite is on the upper level, it needs to be good-sized, offering a sitting area and some nice features in the bath. Buyers need a place to relax on the upper level.

Two-story homes also allow me to create full two-story walls that extend from the lower level. I like to do that as much as possible because the home lines up better structurally. It's a better house from an engineering standpoint. It's also more cost effective to design two-story walls.

—W.L. Martin

PLAN #	PLAN NAME	SQ. FT.	PAGE #
24043	Inverness	1632	94-95
24042	Wedgeport	1689	96-97
24044	Farrelton	1823	98-99
24050	Lemsford	1893	100-101
24054	Westport	1953	102-103
24047	Greenway	2058	104-105
24053	Gearhart	2192	106-107
24049	Dinsmore	2222	108-109
24046	Windor	2284	110-111
24005	Laramie	2497	112-113
24052	Goldendale	3002	114-115

W.L. MARTIN
HOME DESIGNS™

Price Code 16

plan name **INVERNESS**

plan number **#24043-9P**

Three dormers are balanced above a front porch spanning the elevation of this design.

- The living room will accommodate large gatherings and features a fireplace and view to the front.

- In the kitchen, a corner sink has room to grow herbs beneath corner windows.

- An informal dining room both views and accesses the rear yard.

- Walk-in closets for two and a corner soaking tub are included in the master suite.

- Two other bedrooms are comfortably sized for extra furniture, such as toy chests.

Second Floor

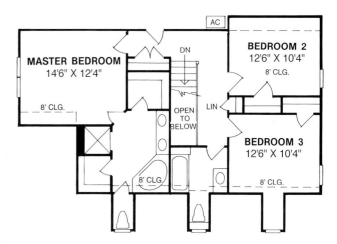

FIRST FLOOR	731
SECOND FLOOR	901
TOTAL SQ. FT.	1632

First Floor

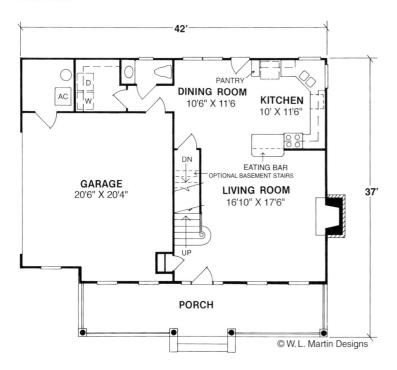

© W. L. Martin Designs

ORDER DIRECT
TOLL-FREE
(800) 947~7526
www.designbasics.com

W.L. MARTIN
HOME DESIGNS™

Price Code 16

plan name **WEDGEPORT**

plan number **#24042-9P**

Four upper-level windows and sidelights bring a feeling of openness to this home's two-story entry.

- Bayed windows offer beauty in the formal dining room, located next to the kitchen.

- An angled eating bar was designed for an informal meal or to serve those in the living room.

- A fireplace accents the rear view in the living room.

- Amenities in the master suite include a walk-in closet, double vanity and whirlpool tub.

- An organized utility area consists of a powder bath and laundry room with soaking sink and counter space for folding clothes.

FIRST FLOOR	979
SECOND FLOOR	710
TOTAL SQ. FT.	1689

Second Floor

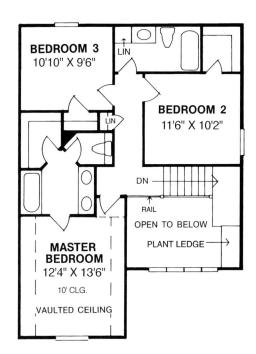

BEDROOM 3
10'10" X 9'6"

LIN

BEDROOM 2
11'6" X 10'2"

DN

RAIL

OPEN TO BELOW

PLANT LEDGE

MASTER BEDROOM
12'4" X 13'6"

10' CLG.

VAULTED CEILING

LIN

First Floor

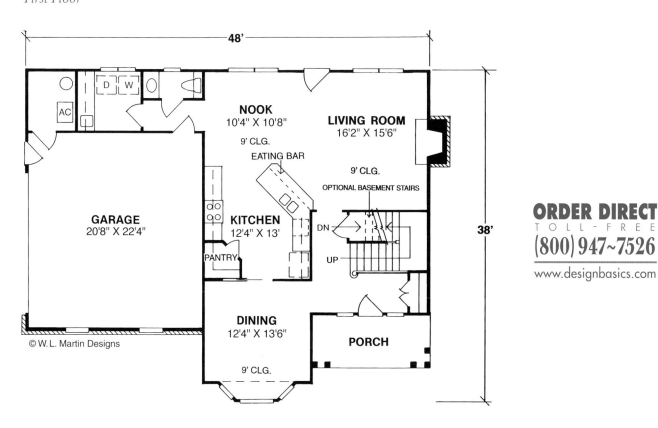

48'

38'

NOOK
10'4" X 10'8"

9' CLG.

EATING BAR

LIVING ROOM
16'2" X 15'6"

9' CLG.

OPTIONAL BASEMENT STAIRS

GARAGE
20'8" X 22'4"

KITCHEN
12'4" X 13'

DN

UP

PANTRY

DINING
12'4" X 13'6"

9' CLG.

PORCH

AC

D W

© W. L. Martin Designs

ORDER DIRECT
TOLL-FREE
(800) 947~7526
www.designbasics.com

97

W.L. MARTIN
HOME DESIGNS™

Price Code 18

plan name **FARRELTON**

plan number **#24044-9P**

This design caters to a variety of needs with a flexible room just inside the entry.

- A pair of double windows brings light into the living room, which features a fireplace.

- The shared space between the kitchen and breakfast nook allows guests to mingle without feeling cramped.

- A rear staircase makes accessing the upper level convenient from either the kitchen area or living room.

- The master bedroom has a raised ceiling and features a walk-in closet and soaking tub.

- Both a powder bath and laundry room are just a short distance from the kitchen.

FIRST FLOOR	1014
SECOND FLOOR	809
TOTAL SQ. FT.	1823

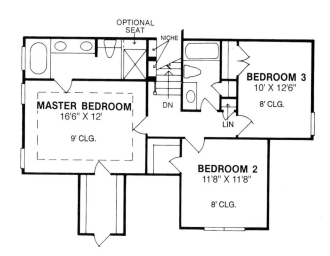

Second Floor

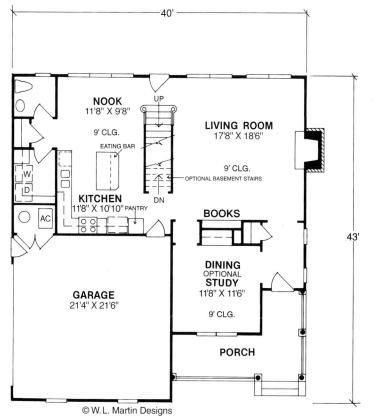

First Floor

© W. L. Martin Designs

ORDER DIRECT
TOLL-FREE
(800) 947~7526
www.designbasics.com

W.L. MARTIN
HOME DESIGNS™

Price Code 19

plan name **LEMSFORD**

plan number **#24050-9P**

The garage and utility area of this home are dressed on the exterior with a brick facing and batten-board shutters.

- Double doors offer privacy in the study, which can also function as a dining room.

- The living room has plenty of light and extends onto a rear porch through a set of French doors.

- The kitchen is positioned to the front of the home and features counters designed in an efficient U-shape.

- The upper level has a sense of airiness, granted from the open railing and mid-level window location on the stairwell.

- The master bedroom is positioned between its walk-in closet and bath with double vanity and whirlpool tub.

FIRST FLOOR	1035
SECOND FLOOR	858
TOTAL SQ. FT.	1893

Second Floor

First Floor

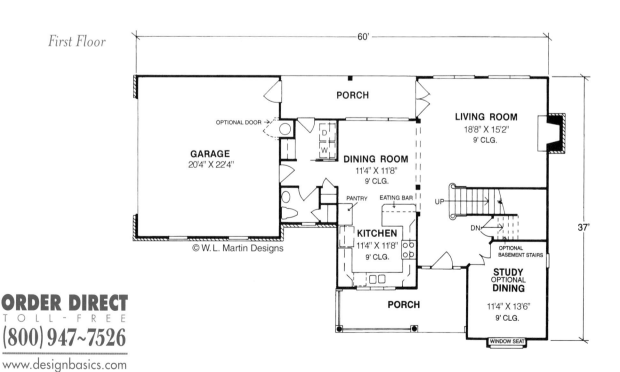

© W. L. Martin Designs

ORDER DIRECT
TOLL-FREE
(800) 947~7526
www.designbasics.com

W.L. MARTIN
HOME DESIGNS™

Price Code 19

plan name **WESTPORT**

plan number **#24054-9P**

WESTPORT

The master suite is adorned with a vaulted ceiling, walk-in closet and double vanity beside a whirlpool tub.

- A pair of identical gable facings draw the eye to the front door, decorated with roof brackets.

- A sense of openness is felt in the entry with its unrestricted view of the dining room and living room.

- The kitchen features a walk-in pantry and eating bar.

- The breakfast nook has direct access to a rear porch.

- A rear staircase leads to a computer nook with plenty of windows providing natural light.

FIRST FLOOR	1020
SECOND FLOOR	933
TOTAL SQ. FT.	1953

ORDER DIRECT
TOLL-FREE
(800) 947~7526
www.designbasics.com

Second Floor

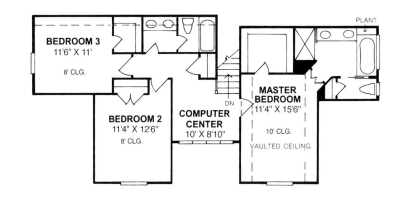

First Floor

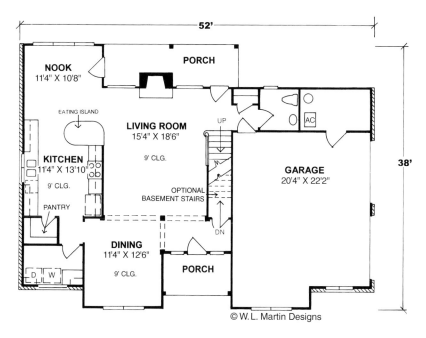

© W. L. Martin Designs

W.L. MARTIN
HOME DESIGNS™

Price Code 20

plan name **GREENWAY**

plan number **#24047-9P**

The dining room has optional use as a study and features bayed windows and columns framing its entry.

- A bayed turret on this home's elevation gives it its castle-like presence.

- Guests can easily circulate in the large living room with fireplace and double windows to the rear.

- A long eating bar in the kitchen can seat the whole family or provide an ideal location to serve a buffet.

- Bedroom 4 makes a charming guest suite with its bayed windows and walk-in closet.

- A double vanity, walk-in closet and whirlpool tub beneath a window serve a large master bedroom with corner windows.

Second Floor

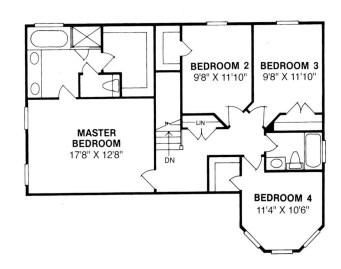

BEDROOM 2
9'8" X 11'10"

BEDROOM 3
9'8" X 11'10"

MASTER BEDROOM
17'8" X 12'8"

LIN

DN

BEDROOM 4
11'4" X 10'6"

First Floor

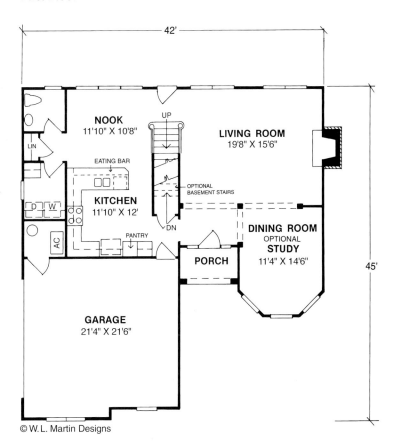

42'

NOOK
11'10" X 10'8"

UP

LIVING ROOM
19'8" X 15'6"

LIN

EATING BAR

OPTIONAL
BASEMENT STAIRS

KITCHEN
11'10" X 12'

D   W

DN

AC

PANTRY

DINING ROOM
OPTIONAL
STUDY
11'4" X 14'6"

PORCH

45'

GARAGE
21'4" X 21'6"

© W. L. Martin Designs

FIRST FLOOR	1008
SECOND FLOOR	1050
TOTAL SQ. FT.	2058

ORDER DIRECT
TOLL-FREE
(800) 947~7526
www.designbasics.com

W.L. MARTIN
HOME DESIGNS™

Price Code 21

plan name **GEARHART**

plan number **#24053-9P**

Paired with a number of windows to each side, an upper-level balcony creates charm on the façade of this home.

- An arched opening leads to a quiet study with a view to the front.

- Opposite the study, an identical arched opening frames a view into the dining room.

- An eating round in the kitchen is a great place to serve snacks or use as an informal eating table.

- On the upper level, the master bath is positioned in an "L" shape around a walk-in closet.

- The garage is discreetly located at the rear of the home.

Second Floor

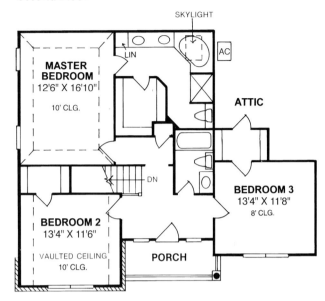

First Floor

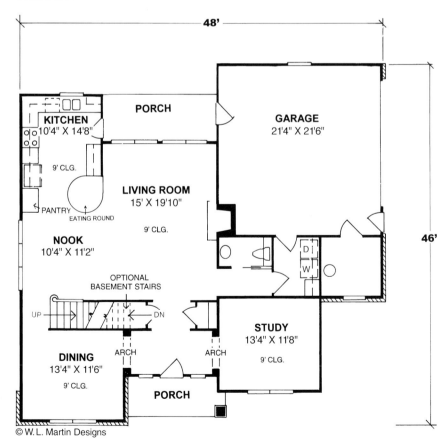

© W. L. Martin Designs

ORDER DIRECT
T O L L - F R E E
(800) 947~7526
www.designbasics.com

FIRST FLOOR	1210
SECOND FLOOR	982
TOTAL SQ. FT.	2192

W.L. MARTIN
HOME DESIGNS™

Price Code 22

plan name **DINSMORE**

plan number **#24049-9P**

A pair of upper-level windows with shutters above equal wings of the front porch, play an important role in balancing this home's elevation.

- The study offers a touch of elegance with columns framing its entry.

- Carrying on the symmetry of the study, columns also frame the dining room, located next to the kitchen.

- While working at the island in the kitchen, enjoy a view onto the rear porch.

- The garage offers a built-in workbench in addition to space for garden storage.

- An upper-level sitting area has view to the front and is accessible from all bedrooms.

FIRST FLOOR	1154
SECOND FLOOR	1068
TOTAL SQ. FT.	2222

Second Floor

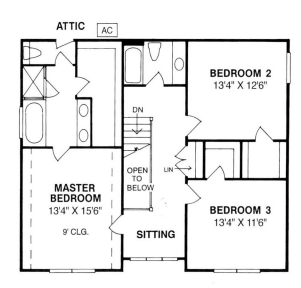

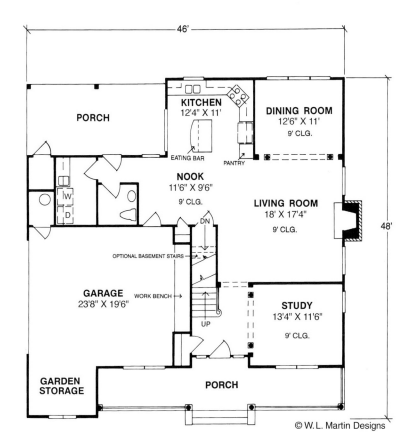

First Floor

ORDER DIRECT
TOLL-FREE
(800) 947~7526
www.designbasics.com

© W. L. Martin Designs

W.L. MARTIN
HOME DESIGNS™

Price Code 22

plan name **WINDOR**

plan number **#24046-9P**

A two-story portico trimmed in traditional scrollwork calls attention to this home's stately design.

- A series of repetitive arches defies the home's traditional roots and creates an impressive vista into the living room.

- The kitchen was meant for cooking, with an island cooktop and corner sink with side view.

- The grand stair hall leads to a quaint balcony that overlooks the front yard.

- Each of three additional bedrooms has a walk-in closet.

- A covered drive-through leads to a rear, two-car garage and offers a sheltered pathway to a third garage stall.

Second Floor

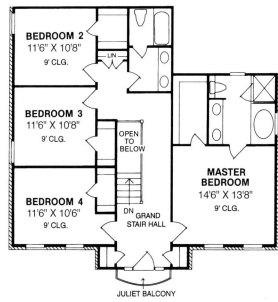

First Floor

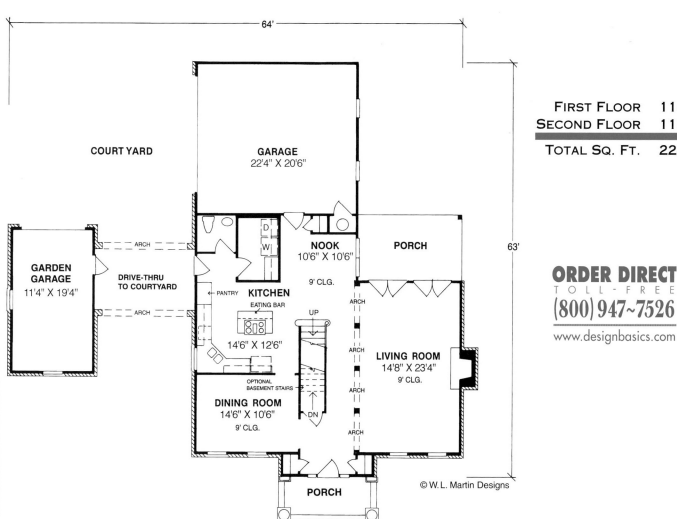

FIRST FLOOR	1148
SECOND FLOOR	1136
TOTAL SQ. FT.	2284

ORDER DIRECT
TOLL-FREE
(800) 947~7526
www.designbasics.com

© W. L. Martin Designs

W.L. MARTIN
HOME DESIGNS™

Price Code 24

plan name **LARAMIE**

plan number **#24005-9P**

Tucking a third stall beneath the front gable helps balance the look of this home's three-car garage.

- The study is designed with a vaulted ceiling and a triple window and can also be utilized as a formal dining room.

- Those relaxing in the living room will be able to enjoy the company of those in the open kitchen and dining room.

- Flex space on the second floor offers use as a playroom or fifth bedroom.

- A walk-in closet, double vanity and vaulted ceiling are features in the master suite.

- A main-floor guest suite is ideally located for privacy.

FIRST FLOOR	1323
SECOND FLOOR	1174
TOTAL SQ. FT.	**2497**

Second Floor

First Floor

© W. L. Martin Designs

ORDER DIRECT
TOLL-FREE
(800) 947~7526
www.designbasics.com

W.L. MARTIN
HOME DESIGNS™

Price Code 30

plan name **GOLDENDALE**

plan number **#24052-9P**

A combination of both brick and siding combine two popular, traditional styles on this home's front elevation.

- Double doors open to the study with bayed windows and close proximity to a main-floor powder bath.

- Windows line the rear of the home, offering a stunning view from the living room and breakfast nook.

- Two covered porches offer a shady alternative to an open-air deck.

- In the master suite, a fireplace is located beneath a vaulted ceiling.

- Bedroom two completes a bayed turret on the home's elevation and offers its own bath and walk-in closet.

Second Floor

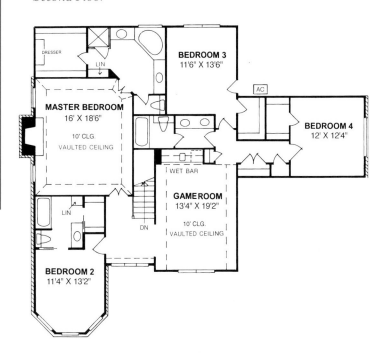

First Floor

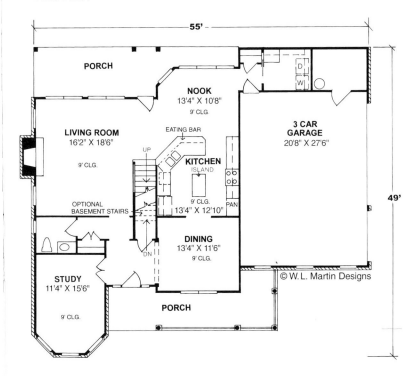

© W. L. Martin Designs

FIRST FLOOR	1303
SECOND FLOOR	1699
TOTAL SQ. FT.	3002

ORDER DIRECT
TOLL-FREE
(800) 947~7526
www.designbasics.com

Every plan CAN BE
CUSTOMIZED ....

CUSTOMIZE
any home plan

If one of these designs is *almost* what
you want, **W.L. Martin** will make it
exactly what you want.

For information on any custom changes,
Call (800) 947-7526
www.designbasics.com

COPYRIGHT
Cans & Cannots

ALL PLANS HAVE BEEN REGISTERED
ORIGINAL
C
DRAFT
WITH THE U.S. COPYRIGHT OFFICE

These days it seems almost everybody has a question about what can or cannot be done
with copyrighted home plans. We know U.S. copyright law can sometimes get complex
and confusing, but here are a few of the basic points of the law you'll want to remember.
Once you've purchased a plan from us and have received a construction license

You Can ...

■ Construct the plan as originally designed,
or change it to meet your specific needs.

■ Build it as many times as you wish *without*
additional re-use fees.

■ Make duplicate blueprint copies as
needed for construction.

**PROTECT YOUR
RIGHTS** to build, modify
and reproduce our home plans with
a construction license.

You Cannot ...

■ Build your plans without a construction license.

■ Copy *any* part of our original designs to create
another design of your own.

■ Claim copyright on changes you make to
our plans.

■ Give a plan to someone else for
construction purposes.

■ Sell the plan.

The above points are provided as general guidelines only.
Additional information is provided with each home plan
purchase, or is available upon request at (800) 947-7526.

There's always something
new going on at Design Basics

Visit Our Website Today!

design basics inc®
HOME PLAN DESIGN SERVICE

(800) 947-7526
FAX: (402) 331-5507

WELCOME TO AMERICA'S #1 HOME PLAN DESIGN SERVICE

Award-winning Designs

Browse hundreds of our award-winning designs with our easy-to-use online search engine.

Monthly Designs

Each month we showcase a design from each of our collections.

DBI Builders

Visit builders in your state who have linked their websites to Design Basics.

Plan Books

Check out our complete library of home design books.

What's New

Find out about new plans and products from Design Basics.

Newspaper Syndication

We now offer an online "Home of the Week" syndication feature that your local newspaper can download and use for free. Make sure you let them know.

Industry Links

Potential buyers can visit your site. We receive over **two million** hits per month. You can't afford *not* to be here.

Construction Alternatives

Discover the possibilities of panelized construction.

Common Questions

Find answers to the most commonly asked questions about our designs.

TO SEE THIS HOME OR OTHER HOME PLANS, VISIT US AT:

www.designbasics.com
E-mail: info@designbasics.com

Space Planning PRODUCTS & SERVICES

Great Ways to Simplify Your Life

For many home buyers, visualizing the finished home is a challenge. Our Study Print & Furniture Layout Guide™ makes it easy. First, the **Study Print provides views of all exterior elevations.** Secondly, the **Furniture Layout Guide provides a "Feel" for room sizes,** with a 1/4" scale floor plan, over 100 reusable furniture pieces and helpful tips on space planning.

– Available for any W.L. Martin plan –

only $29.95

STUExDY PRINT & FURNITURE LAYOUT GUIDE™

Specifications & Finishing
CHECKLIST™

With this handy **reference tool** you'll never forget the little things. Each decision you need to make during the construction of your home is outlined in an easy-to-follow format. Everything from the types of excavation to the brand and style of doorknobs.

No builder or consumer should be without the Specifications & Finishing Checklist™ from Design Basics.

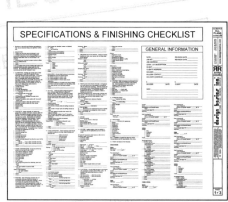

18" x 24" Format

CHOOSE EITHER FORM

8 1/2" x 11" Format

Call 800|947|7526 To Order

$14.95 **EACH**

DESIGN BASICS' HOME PLAN LIBRARY

17.

16.

1.

2.

3.

1) Impressions of Home™
Homes designed with the look you want – 100 designs from 1339' to 4139'. $4.95

2) Impressions of Home™
Homes designed for the way you live – 100 designs from 1191' to 4228'. $4.95

3) Heartland Home Plans™
120 plan ideas designed for everyday practicality. Warm, unpretentious elevations easily adapt to individual lifestyles. From 1212' to 2631'. $8.95

4) Reflections of an American Home™ Vol. III
50 photographed home plans with warm remembrances of home and beautiful interior presentations. From 1341' to 3775'. $4.95

5) Photographed Portraits of an American Home™
100 of our finest designs, beautifully photographed and tastefully presented among charming photo album memories of "home." A must for any sales center's coffee table. $14.95

6) Gold Seal™ Home Plan Book Set – 442 of today's most sought-after one-story, 1 ½ story and 2-story home plan ideas. All 5 books for $84.95 or $19.95 each

- Homes of Distinction – 86 plans under 1800'
- Homes of Sophistication – 106 plans, 1800'-2199'
- Homes of Elegance – 107 plans, 2200'-2599'
- Homes of Prominence – 75 plans, 2600'-2999'
- Homes of Grandeur – 68 plans, 3000'-4000'

7) Timeless Legacy™, A Collection of Fine Home Designs by Carmichael & Dame – 52 breathtaking luxury home designs from 3300' to 4500'. Includes artful rear views of each home. $25.00

8) The Homes of Carmichael & Dame™ Vol. II
60 elegant designs from simple to sublime. From 1751' to 4228'. $9.95

9) *Seasons of Life™
Designs for Reaping the Rewards of Autumn
100 home plans specially tailored to today's empty-nester. From 1212' to 3904'. $4.95

10) *Seasons of Life™
Designs for Living Summer's Journey – 100 designs for the move-up buyer. From 1605' to 3775'. $4.95

11) *Seasons of Life™
Designs for Spring's New Beginnings – 100 home plans for first-time buyers. Presentations unique to this lifestyle. From 1125' to 2537'. $4.95

12) W.L. Martin Home Designs™
53 beautiful home plans offering outstanding livability. From 1262' to 3914'. $9.95

13) The Narrow Home Plan™ Collection
258 one-story, 1 ½ story and 2-story home plans that are from 26 to 50 feet wide. This book also includes 25 duplex plans. $14.95

14) Nostalgia Home Plans Collection™
A New Approach to Time-Honored Design
70 designs showcasing enchanting details and unique "special places." From 1339' to 3480'. $9.95

15) Nostalgia Home Plans Collection™ Vol. II
A New Approach to Time-Honored Design
70 designs bringing back the essence of homes of the past. $9.95

16) Gold Seal Favorites™ – 100 best selling plans from the famous Gold Seal™ Collection, including 25 duplex designs. $6.95

17) Easy Living One-Story Designs™
155 one-story home designs from the Gold Seal™, Heartland Home Plans™ and Timeless Legacy™ collections, together in one plan book. $7.95

*Order the complete Seasons of Life™ set (all three books) for only $9.00

15.

14.

13.

12.

ORDER DIRECT
TOLL-FREE
(800) 947~7526
www.designbasics.com

5.

6.

7.

8.

11.

10.

9.

9P

A PLAN FROM W.L. MARTIN: WHAT'S IN IT FOR YOU?

Plans come to you on high-quality reproducible vellums and include the following:

COVER PAGE Each W.L. Martin home plan features the front elevation and informative reference sections including: general notes and design criteria.

ELEVATIONS Drafted at ¼" scale for the front and ⅛" scale for the rear and sides. All elevations are detailed and an aerial view of the roof is provided, showing all hips, valleys, ridges and framing.

FOUNDATIONS Drafted at ¼" scale. Basement, slab and crawl space foundations are included.

MAIN LEVEL FLOOR PLAN Drafted at ¼" scale. 2"x4" walls are standard. The detailed drawings include such things as ceiling treatments and header locations.

SECOND LEVEL FLOOR PLAN Drafted at ¼" scale. Drafted to the same degree of detail as the main level floor plan.*

INTERIOR ELEVATIONS Kitchen cabinet elevations are drawn.

ELECTRICAL AND SECTIONS The electrical plan shows suggested electrical layout for the main and second level floor plans. Typical wall, stair, brick sections are provided to further explain construction of these areas.

All plan orders received prior to 2:00 p.m. CT will be processed, inspected and shipped out the same afternoon via 2nd business day air within the continental United States. All other product orders will be sent via UPS ground service. Full Technical Support is available for any plan purchase from W.L. Martin. Our Technical Support Specialists provide unlimited technical support free of charge and answer questions regarding construction methods, framing techniques and more. **Please call 800-947-7526 for more information.**

CONSTRUCTION LICENSE

When you purchase a W.L. Martin home plan, you receive a Construction License w gives you certain rights in building the home depicted in that plan, including:

NO RE-USE FEE As the original purchaser of a W.L. Martin home plan Construction License permits you to build the plan as many times as you like.

LOCAL MODIFICATIONS The Construction License allows you to make modifica to your W.L. Martin plans. We offer a complete custom change service, or you may hav desired changes done locally by a qualified draftsman, designer, architect or engineer.

RUNNING BLUEPRINTS If your plans are sent to you on vellum paper the reproduce well on your blueprint machine. The Construction License authorizes y your blueprint facility, at your direction, to make as many copies of the plan from th lum masters as you need for construction purposes.

*This plan was designed and drafted by W.L. Martin Home Designs to meet average con and codes in the state of Oklahoma at the time it was designed. Because codes and regu can change and may vary from jurisdiction to jurisdiction, W.L. Martin Home Designs warrant compliance with any special code or regulation. Consult your local building offi determine the suitability of these plans for your specific site and application.

This plan can be adapted to your local building codes and requirements, but also, it responsibility of the purchaser and/or builder of this plan to see that the structure is built compliance with all governing municipal codes (city, state and federal).

TO ORDER DIRECT: CALL 800-947-7526 • MONDAY – FRIDAY 7:00 a.m. – 6:00 p.m. CT

Name _____

Address _____
(For UPS Delivery – Packages cannot be shipped to a P.O. Box.)

Above Address: ☐ business address   ☐ residence address

☐ VISA [VISA]   ☐ MasterCard [MasterCard]
We appreciate it when you use VISA or MasterCard.

Credit Card: ☐☐☐☐☐☐☐☐☐☐☐☐☐☐☐☐

☐ Check enclosed   ☐ AMEX   ☐ Discover

Signature _____

Company _____

Title _____

City _____   State _____   Zip_____

Phone (___) _____   FAX (___) _____

Expiration Date: ☐☐ / ☐☐

✔	HOME PLAN PRODUCTS	PLAN #	QTY.	PRICE	SHIPPING & HANDLING	TOTAL
☐	1 Set of Master Vellum Prints or 5 Sets of Blueprints					$
☐	Add'l. Sets of Blueprints – $20.00					$
☐	Study Print & Furniture Layout Guide™ - $29.95 (if available)					$
☐	Specifications & Finishing Checklist™ - $14.95					$
☐						$
☐						$

BOOK NUMBER   • BOOK NAME

☐	Complete Plan Book Library – $150.00					$
						$
						$

• CALL FOR • Shipping & Handling Charges

• No COD Orders • US Funds Only •
NO REFUNDS OR EXCHANGES, PLEASE

Subtotal $

NE Residents Add 6.5% Sales Tax $

Total $

CALL 800-947-7526
OR MAIL ORDER TO: **Design Basics**
11112 John Galt Blvd.
Omaha, NE 68137

PRICES SUBJECT TO CHANGE

PLAN PRICE SCHEDULE

Plan Price Code	Total Sq. Ft.	Plan Pric
12	1200' - 1299'	$505
13	1300' - 1399'	$515
14	1400' - 1499'	$525
15	1500' - 1599'	$535
16	1600' - 1699'	$545
17	1700' - 1799'	$555
18	1800' - 1899'	$565
19	1900' - 1999'	$575
20	2000' - 2099'	$585
21	2100' - 2199'	$595
22	2200' - 2299'	$605
23	2300' - 2399'	$615
24	2400' - 2499'	$625
25	2500' - 2599'	$635
26	2600' - 2699'	$645
27	2700' - 2799'	$655
28	2800' - 2899'	$665
29	2900' - 2999'	$675
30	3000' - 3099'	$685
38	3800' - 3899'	$765
39	3900' - 3999'	$775